DATE DUE

DEMCO 38-296

Edward Schreiner

Backpacking
With Babies
& Small Children

A guide to taking the kids along
on day hikes, overnighters,
and long trail trips

Goldie Silverman

WILDERNESS PRESS
BERKELEY

abies and Small Children

Book design by Jaan Hitt
Cover design by Jaan Hitt
Cover photos by Vern Clevenger

Library of Congress Catalog Number 98-8596
ISBN 0-89997-239-X

Printed in the United States of America
Published by: Wilderness Press
              2440 Bancroft Way
              Berkeley, CA 94704
              (800) 443-7227
              FAX (510) 548-1355
              mail@wildernesspress.com

              Contact us for a free catalog
              Visit our web site at www.wildernesspress.com

 Printed on recycled paper, 20% post-consumer waste

Library of Congress Cataloging-in-Publication Data

Silverman, Goldie.
    Backpacking with babies and small children: a guide to taking
the kids long on day hikes, overnighters, and long trips/ Goldie
Silverman. -3rd ed.
          p.   cm.
    Includes bibliography references (p.) and index.
    ISBN 0-89997-239-X (alk. paper)
    1. Backpacking. 2. Family recreation. I Title.
GV199.6.S54 1998
796.51-dc21
                                        98-8596
                                        CIP

CONTENTS

PREFACE

When I think about the hikes that my husband and I have taken, exploring beaches, forests, and mountains, first with the children, then by ourselves, and now with three generations, I realize that these have been some of the best times of our lives.

We came late to backpacking. When we first moved to the Northwest and learned that hiking was what people did, we had enormous feelings of regret. We already had three children. We thought it was too late for us to begin. But we did begin, and we learned as we went, step by step, taking the children along until they were grown and faster than we were and off on their own. We bought a smaller tent and continued. Then there were grandchildren to hike with us, until they too will be off on their own!

Our family took our first hiking trip in 1966, when our youngest, a plump fifteen-month-old, was not yet walking. It was a disaster. We chose our destination from a guide book: a lake 9 miles away by trail that had an elevation gain of 2000 feet to reach it. We constructed a seat for the baby by lashing his plastic infant's seat, without its pad, to a homemade wooden Trapper Nelson-type packframe. Thick straps held baby, seat, and frame together. My husband carried this 42-pound combination.

The other children—ages six and eight—and I were outfitted at an army surplus store. On our backs we wore heavy canvas bags of varying shapes and sizes, held in place with makeshift arrangements of narrow cotton straps. Round our waists we wore thick webbed belts, from which we suspended canteens in rugged cloth cases. The children filled their bags with toys, and I carried everything else for the day. At least we were wise enough not to try an overnighter for our first experience.

The guide book said there was water on the trail, so we did not fill our canteens at home. None of us realized that the long hot summer we were having would have dried up the streams we were supposed to find. In a very short time, we were all hot and thirsty. The straps cut into our shoulders and the canteens banged our sides. We turned back after only an hour.

Next week we tried again. This time our destination was a lake only 1 mile from the road, with an elevation gain of about 50 feet. The big kids carried one toy apiece in their bags, with some of the food and their own sweaters. Mom and Dad wore the belts with the dangling canteens, and the canteens were full. We had a wonderful day, with Bench Lake all to ourselves and Mount Rainier across the valley as our own glorious personal mountain. We've been hiking ever since, and what we've learned can help your family start hiking without having to go through disastrous first experiences.

Perhaps you have been an avid outdoors person all your life, and now that you have produced an infant, you don't want to give up all your outdoor interests while you wait for the child to be able to do his or her share of the work on expeditions. Or maybe, like us, you have never hiked or backpacked, but now you have a family of two or three kids under the age of eight, and you think hiking might be a good activity that the whole family can enjoy. It's healthy, it's cheap, and it's supposed to be spiritually uplifting as well. You may have read a book or two on backpacking, or even taken a course. You have an idea of how you yourself should begin, but nothing you have learned has shown you how to include the children.

This book is for people like you—people who want to hike and backpack with their babies and small children. It is not a handbook of how to go backpacking; there are plenty of other books to tell you that, and you should certainly have one of them as a reference. This book begins where those other books leave off; it will tell you how to take the kids along.

This is the third edition of *BACKPACKING WITH BABIES AND SMALL CHILDREN*, following the second in 1986 and the first in 1975. At risk of sounding like an old curmudgeon, nattering on about how much harder life was in the old days, I can't resist pointing out how much easier it is for parents to backpack with their children in 1998 than it was in 1986 and certainly in 1975. To cite some of the improvements, parents today can select from among many different models of child carriers and packs for kids, they can buy stylish raingear for their children, they can find sturdy child-sized clothing that is warm when wet. In the first edition, I devoted a lot of space to improvising or making all such gear. No makeshift carriers for you! Nor do you have to put your toddler's legs through the sleeves of mom's polypropylene undershirt to improvise long johns.

As I collected information about all the new equipment and materials that are available for hiking with kids today, I thought about leaving those sections out of the third edition. I thought maybe today's reader wouldn't be interested in making-do with homemade equipment. Unless, of course, you, dear reader, aren't sure you're willing or able to invest a bundle to take the family out for a weekend of activity that you may not like at all. Even though wonderful gear may be available, not everyone will want to outfit the family with all the necessities at once. Furthermore, there is a great satisfaction in creating your own equipment; part of the enjoyment of your expeditions should be the anticipation and planning of your trip. As you think about some of the problems you might encounter, you might let your own solutions and inventions be part of that enjoyment. So the making-do parts remain in the book.

What I learned through the years is in this book, but that's not all that's in it. Over the years, I have appealed to hikers through magazines and newsletters, and just by accosting families on the trail, to ask them how they manage backpacking with their children. When I give talks at trails expos, I always ask what parents want in a book like mine. For this revision, I hung around at the play area of an outdoors store on Saturday mornings, asking people, What do you do with your kids? How do you do it? I think of these people as my resources. One amazing thing I have discovered in talking to a lot of different people is the enormous diversity in the ways we all do the same things. People are wonderful, and they show it in the uniquely personal way each one handles a similar problem. There is no one right way to take the kids backpacking. This book will not tell you how to camp like Goldie Silverman does; it will tell you several different ways that other families have solved problems so that you can choose your own way from among them, the one that is best for your family.

The book begins with a general guide to planning family hikes. The next seven chapters deal with what to take, not just listing the items you will need, but telling you how to choose them, where to look for them, how to use them, and, in some cases, how to dispose of them. The last three chapters tell you what to do, on the trail and in camp, to keep your children safe and contented. Appendices will list additional resources for equipment and advice.

In the earlier editions, in an attempt to be egalitarian, I referred to my resources as *parents, boy, girl* or *child* as in "One parent told me that her son...." I also tried to avoid the first person. Those practices now strike me as unfriendly. I know that the common English practice of using the pronoun *he* to refer to neutral nouns like *child* offends many mothers of daughters (myself included), but I find usages like *he/she* cumbersome. I solved those problems in this book by sometimes giving names to my resources, by appearing in my own character more frequently, and by using the forms of *she* and *he* to refer to the noun *child*, in alternating chapters. Because it has been many years since I spoke to some of my resources and I can't always identify who said what, I have not tried to use the actual names but have borrowed first names from friends and family. If anyone is offended by the words I seem to have assigned to them, I apologize, but remind them that I know many people with similar first names!

PART I

PLANNING YOUR TRIP

STARTING ON THE RIGHT FOOT

A **famous writer once said that all happy families are alike.**
That may be true in stories, but it certainly isn't true among backpackers. Families who hike and backpack successfully have learned that what works for one family and makes them happy may be all wrong for another.

Imagine a trailhead with three parties about to set out, each with two adults and some children. In the first family, let's call them the Steadies, everyone adjusts his pace to what the youngest walker can do. Over the years, Mom Steady has concluded that no matter what the circumstances, no matter what the terrain, children under the age of six cannot travel more than one mile per hour. When the Steady family hikes, they have frequent stops to admire nature, to ask questions, to take a drink, to eat a Lifesaver®. Sometimes they turn back before they reach their destination. Sometimes they set up camp at the first pleasant spot they see, instead of pressing on to their intended goal. No one ever feels the need to cover a lot of miles and everyone has a relaxed, comfortable time.

The Zoomer family would never go hiking with the Steadies. One of the Zoomers, let's say the dad, likes to move! As far as he is concerned, a day of strolling is a day wasted. When the Zoomers set out in the morning, they leave one heavy pack behind them! Mom takes a light day pack with the essentials for herself and the children. Dad with his heavy pack zooms ahead of the rest of the family. He reaches their next campsite, leaves the first pack, returns to their previous camp, and shoulders the second pack. When he overtakes his family, he may join them for the last leg of the trip, but more likely he will hurry on to set up camp before they arrive. Sometimes the kids get tired and leave their packs on the trail; Dad goes back for those too. Mr. Zoomer travels many times as far as the rest of the family. Although he doesn't spend his second night as far from his first night's camp as he might have BC (Before Children), he has still covered the same distance on foot.

Neither of these plans would work for the Even family. Both these parents like to cover ground, but they also want to be fair to their children and to each other. When the Evens backpack, they set up a base camp a day's walk into the wilderness. On some days they take short dayhikes all together, and on other days the parents take turns staying with the children and hiking off alone. Some days one parent will hike back to the car for more supplies. The Evens both like the solitude of hiking alone, and their children are happier when they're not being pushed. They don't have to break camp every morning, and if the weather changes they can get back to their car quickly.

Which family has developed the plan that would be right for you? No one can decide that except you. If you have never hiked

A happy hiker, ready to go

Jeffrey Hancock

with your own family members, you may want to try all three, or some combination of the three.

Single parents who are reading this book may already feel angry at the assumption that every child will have *two* parents to take him hiking. Of course that isn't always true; there are some children with only one parent, and there are some families in which only one parent will want to go hiking. But caring for yourself *and* for a young child in the woods can be a lot of work. Sometimes it's more work than one person can handle. Who will cook dinner while your toddler explores the campsite? Who will go for help if you are hurt? A single parent should ask a co-operative adult friend who knows and likes his child to go along on the adventure, even if it's only a dayhike.

On the other hand, don't take your child along on a hike organized by an outdoor club unless you're positive it's an excursion for families. It's simply not fair to other people to slow them down with your child. They may have gone to some trouble to leave their own children at home. Even if the outing is intended as a family affair, don't expect the others to help you care for your child. The outdoor life is supposed to teach self-sufficiency.

An ocean beach was this baby's first camp

James Evans

Joining a hiking club is a good way to learn backpacking techniques. So is taking a course; there are lots of courses in backpacking for adults. For starters, look at the offerings of your local community college, park department, and Y's, or call your branch of the Sierra Club or a local outdoor club. Ask your library or the sports department of your newspaper to help you find a class. Look on the Internet. But if you join an adult group to learn to hike, leave the kids at home. Then when you take your family out, you can impress them with your new expertise, and you won't be holding back anyone else.

Parents who take their children on outdoor excursions must expect to make some concessions and adjustments, but there are rewards, too, especially as children become aware of the natural world around them. Every hike should be an adventure. You can share with your children the special feeling of self-sufficiency, of managing with just the material goods you can carry; you and they can enjoy the companionship of the people you like best, without the distractions and interruptions of the outside world. All of you can appreciate the natural beauty of the area you choose to explore, and the hint of what all of our cities and suburbs looked like to the earliest people who lived there. And all of you can relax the day-to-day standards of cleanliness and propriety, get dirty and stay dirty, and have fun!

People who hike, children included, do tend to get dirty. Even babies in carriers get dirtier in the woods than they do at home. Happy children are allowed to stay dirty. Of course, parents will try to see that everyone eats with relatively clean hands, but otherwise no one should expect to maintain the same standards on the trail that exist in the home. A person who tries to bring his home with him to the woods will be very dissatisfied and unhappy. He may also find himself with a very heavy pack!

Think of all that you're missing if you don't go. Then stop just thinking, make your plans, and go!

FIRST HIKES

If you have never hiked before, your first trip should not be a long weekend backpack. There are many adjustments to make and much equipment to try out before a family of novice hikers undertakes an overnighter. You want your children to enjoy this experience; therefore it should be exciting and new without being overwhelming.

Lay the foundations for good hiking experiences long before you take to the trail. Encourage small everyday adventures around the house and the neighborhood. "Hike" to the park, the library, or the shopping center. Tell your child what a good hiker he is becoming, and talk about the special hikes the family will take together.

No matter how eager your family is to spend a night in the wild, start them out with simple dayhikes. There will be lots of new experiences: walking on a trail; drinking from a canteen or a special hiker's cup; wearing a pack, perhaps, or at least eating a lunch that was carried in a pack.

You will be testing the plans you made at home. How do your ideas actually work out when you're away from home? Is this a good terrain for kids? Is your destination reasonable? Does every member of the family have the right clothes? Are you prepared for changes in the weather? Do you all have adequate boots or shoes? How do your packs feel? What have you carried along that you don't really need, and, more important, what do you need that you have neglected to bring?

On your very first hike, you will have many details to check. It may be wise to carry a lunch that's all ready to eat, like sandwiches, so that you don't have to worry about new cooking techniques in

Ready for a Father's Day hike

Goldie Silverman

addition to everything else. Then when you know your clothes and packs are right, you can graduate to fixing soup or coffee on the trail. Next you may try a trip preparing two meals out-of-doors, then three, and finally you will be ready for your first overnighter.

Look upon the first overnight trip as a field test of your equipment. You will be completely dependent on the contents of your packs. Many families have taken their first overnight backpacking "trip" in a drive-in campground. They parked their cars outside the campground, walked to a campsite, and lived for a night out of the packs they carried in. On their second trip they were ready to hike away from other people.

Of course, if you have been hiking for years and years without children and you're now starting to take your child with you, you won't have to go through all these steps. All you have to do is to think through the way you care for your child at home and decide how you will do those same tasks out on the trail. You will probably want to try out your new techniques with your baby on a dayhike before you try an overnighter, just to be sure that everything works.

AGE TO START

What age is a good age to start taking your children hiking? That all depends on you. A baby in a pack is a real icebreaker with other hikers along the trail. The babies themselves seem to enjoy being out-of-doors, seeing the sky and the moving trees and other people met along the way. Some parents wait until the baby is strong enough to ride steadily in the carrier and to appreciate the activity and the environment around him. Other parents tell me that they have successfully backpacked with infants as young as three weeks. American Indian babies roamed the Plains in cradleboards shortly after birth. Some years ago a young woman gave birth to her first child in a sleeping bag on a remote beach in Washington State. That infant, who was carried out by his parents the next day, must have set some kind of record among backpackers.

Those parents had no choice, but for the rest of us, good sense must be our guide. A happy, healthy baby, kept warm and dry, can go almost anywhere. Hiking with a baby who is supersensitive and nervous (just like hiking with an adult of similar nature) may prove to be impossible for all but the most patient of parents. A sickly baby should probably stay close to good medical care. Parents who have any doubts about taking their infants anywhere should discuss their concerns with their baby's doctor. Some conservative physicians may reject the whole idea of taking the baby hiking. It helps if parents who want to backpack choose doctors who are backpackers. Don't be afraid to ask if your doctor has experienced hiking with a baby when you ask for his or her advice.

Hiking with toddlers probably presents more problems than hiking with kids of any other age group. Toddlers are heavy to carry, but they are slow walkers. Families with toddlers generally decide upon a combination of carrying and walking. When Jen was in the "terrible twos," the stage where she was asserting her independence in everything, her father told me she would resist either mode of travel if a parent suggested it. They had to let her think she was the one who decided when she walked and when she rode. They tried to distract her from argument by guessing what might be just ahead on the trail. And yet, Jen's father said, two was the best age for hiking with Jen because she was such a good companion. Other ideas for motivation on the trail will be found in the chapter called "Getting There is Half the Fun."

DESTINATIONS

Parents who hike with only an infant in a carrier have at least one advantage over parents who hike with small children: most infants don't have strong feelings about their destinations, whereas small children do. Many parents who hike with young children have learned that a destination that is only a fantastic viewpoint is not an adequate goal for a child. Children don't care about scenery. High up on a ridge, Lynette was disappointed and bored. "Why did we come here?" she asked. "Nothing but lamb-scapes."

Children like fun things, like throwing rocks into water. Good destinations for families with children are lakes, meadows, and river banks. Of course, parents must use good judgment. A high bank with an abrupt dropoff to deep water is not a place to stop with children, and wet rocks alongside a waterfall are dangerous for anyone to climb on. But children can find lots to do beside a wide, low bank or a pebbly beach.

Goldie Silverman

Children like to walk near water

Lake and ocean beaches are good places for hikes with children. The walking is generally easy, and the shoreline provides all sorts of interesting flotsam and jetsam to ponder over and play with. On a beach hike you don't need a destination; the beach is both the trail and the goal.

Some families find that walking near water, such as on a trail that runs alongside a creek, keeps their kids more interested than a trail through deep forest. Others report that their child had been fascinated by a trail which they would have described as "in bad shape." My son John at age four walked 3 miles through a dripping rain forest on a very muddy board walk in Olympic National Park. When he stepped on the end of a board, the other end went up. As he crossed the board, the high end went down with a muddy splash and the back end came up. We heard not one word of complaint through that whole hike. Later he spoke of this memorable day as his best and muddiest hike.

When you plan your hike, and especially if you are planning an overnighter, call or write ahead or stop by the ranger station to get the latest information on the area. Roads and trails wash out or are closed for construction; popular areas may be closed to allow re-vegetation. If you plan to stay overnight, ask about requirements for choosing a campsite, for toileting, and for storing food. Find out if permits are required, and if you must camp at an assigned backcountry campsite. When you set out, be sure to sign the register at the trailhead.

ENDURANCE AND DISTANCES

There are no hard and fast rules that tell you how far a child can go in a day. When you plan a hike with children, you have to stop thinking in terms of how far you can go; instead, begin thinking about how long you want to be on the trail.

Since the time he was two, Walt and Ellyn have expected their son to walk all by himself, without being carried. Now he is five, and his parents report that in three years their speed has not improved. They still average one-half mile per hour. This is the pattern that this family has evolved: they choose fairly strenuous hikes of 3 to 4 miles per day, with 1500 to 2000 feet of elevation gain; they take lots of rest stops; they get a very early start in the morning; they spend a long day on the trail; and they never hike with other families because they don't want to hold anyone else back.

Other children's endurance may not be a good measure of what your children can do. Your six-year-old daughter may go much farther without complaining than my child who is the same age. A family that carries their child some of the time or one that always goes out with friends will have an entirely different profile from the family above. Families learn their own limitations through experience—another good reason for starting out with easy dayhikes. Just remember when you plan your trips that it takes energy to go *up*. You must allow for elevation gain as well as total distance covered. Your general backpacking handbook can help you calculate how elevation gain equates to distance and energy required.

SUPPORTED HIKES

Although many hikers consider the challenge of carrying a week's or more food, shelter, and clothing on their backs an essential element of a wilderness excursion, parents of one or two children may find the challenge overwhelming and give up. These parents should consider a trip with some sort of pack support. Horses, burros, or llamas can be used to carry some or all of the baggage for many days in the wilderness. The animals' owners rent them out in different ways. Some packers will carry many pounds of gear into a base camp while the hikers walk in; after a set number of days, the packer returns, and they all move out. Or the packers and their animals may stay with the clients throughout the trip, moving often. Or a family may take the animals out on their own and be responsible for them.

The most successful trip they ever took, a young mother of two reported, was a three-family trip with burro support. The burros not only carried most of the baggage but also some of the youngsters. The babies in their party rode in backpack carriers while their older siblings traveled two to a burro.

In the Olympic National Park in Washington, we met a family who had brought a pair of llamas from Oregon by trailer. Parents and llamas were loaded for ten days in the park, while two small children carried tiny packs.

If the idea of a hike supported by livestock appeals to you but you don't know where to go for information, search the Internet or write to the capital of the state where you plan to hike. Address your letter to the office of tourism or write to the governor; that office will see that your letter is channeled to the right

A donkey can carry two children

Robert Judson

place. Check to be sure that pack animals are allowed in the areas you plan to visit. Some parts of national parks are closed to stock, while in others there are restrictions on numbers of animals or on grazing. Write or call the park headquarters for information. Start making your plans several months in advance; it takes time to put all the details together.

A bicycle is another form of support. Some young parents take their children on long bicycle tours over backroads, stopping at campgrounds along the way where they can leave the bikes and go off on dayhikes. The child can ride in a seat attached to a parent's bike or in a trailer pulled behind. A good trailer provides protection from wind and rain, and has a plastic window so the child can see out. Panniers on the bikes allow the parents to carry more weight than they could in backpacks, and the route along roads allows them to take advantage of grocery stores and other amenities. But bicycling with children is slower than cycling with adult friends; one couple reported that they could travel only twenty to thirty miles per day when they had their young son along. When they stopped, they wanted to rest, but their son was tired of sitting and wanted to run; they developed a pattern of stopping for exercise breaks for him, and those stops cut down their daily mileage.

Good, strong friends and grandparents can provide a lot of support, too. If one parent carries the baby and some of the gear, the rest of their goods can be divided among two or more other adults. Grandparents might be willing to stay in camp with the kids while parents go off for the heights. Just be sure when you invite friends along that they understand what you expect of them.

FLEXIBLE PLANNING

Parents should keep their plans flexible. Sometimes for unforeseen reasons a planned hike just doesn't work out; if so, the excursion need not become a total loss. A simpler alternative to the cancelled hike can save the day for the whole family. Almost every family that shared its ideas for this book had stories to tell of last-minute changes they had to make in their plans, but if you can't find another option, don't be afraid to turn back.

The Greens had parked their car in a campground prepared to hike to a more remote campsite three miles away by trail. As they unloaded the car, Marge discovered she had forgotten her hiking boots. She had nothing for her feet but the sandals she liked to wear while driving. Instead of turning back or trying to hike in skimpy sandals, they spent the two days as drive-in campers. It was not the same weekend, but it was a good weekend.

Other families report that they were sometimes turned back from hikes into high country by heavy rain, impossible mosquitoes, or a kid with a "stomach ache." They kept the day from being a total failure by camping in a lowland campground, by stopping to explore a quaint small town that they had always whizzed by, or by visiting a fish hatchery or museum that was on the road back.

When it's raining on one side of a mountain, it's sometimes dry on the other. The Walters reached the trailhead of their first choice only to find rain pouring down in sheets, but they had been flexible enough to plan a second choice. They drove a few miles farther over a pass and found splendid, sunny weather on the dry slope. They had left word with their "home guard," the person who would sound the alarm if they did not get home on schedule, that they might be at the second destination, so they felt confident about changing their plans.

Teen-age Juli, who started backpacking at the age of five, told her parents, "I'm sick of hearing 'flexible.' Can't you think of some other word?" But there is no better word.

THE UNHAPPY CHILD

When a child has spent a day in the open air, when the usual rules about a clean face or eating with a fork have been relaxed enough to keep him comfortable, when he has been to a new place and shared a new experience with his family, he has had a wonderful first trip. If his first trip is happy and pleasant, he will be enthusiastic about future trips. But what happens if, for reasons beyond a parent's control, a child's first hiking experience is not a happy one. What can you do with the child who doesn't want to hike?

Some parents report that they would never go out without another family. They have found that the company of other children makes the trip enjoyable for their own offspring. Without these companions, their own children are unbearable. Taking another family also gives adult companionship to the parents. Two truly compatible families hiking together can have a wonderful time. But when families hike together, it is very important that they share similar attitudes toward their adventure. The Zoomers who like to cover ground should not go out with a family of strollers. A long hike together is better undertaken with old friends who know and understand your family than with new acquaintances.

In many families, the children are allowed to ask a friend to go along on dayhikes. Some parents always head for the hills with twice as many kids as they have produced. There are several benefits to taking these guests along: the host children behave better, the guest children have an experience that their own parents may not provide, and the children entertain each other, so the parents who lead the expedition have more time for themselves. Naturally you won't invite a child who is difficult to handle; the guest who doesn't follow "house rules" in your home will be impossible on the trail.

The child who is reluctant to go hiking poses a special problem for the family. Sometimes parents must make a decision based on the degree of the reluctance. If the child's feelings are strong, perhaps he should be left at home. If he enjoys being with his family but is less than enthusiastic about hiking, he can still go along on the hike. He will probably do a minimum share of the work around camp and not carry a pack. Lots of kids' packs get to camp in or on their parents' packs. It may not be fair to the person who has to carry more than his share, but if a child who is going along just for the sake of the family becomes more unhappy, he'll make the whole family miserable!

Children who are really balky and cross about going should be left at home. Find a friend or neighbor who has a child of the same age and leave your kid with them. Promise them that they can retaliate some day when they want to go away without their child.

Then when everyone is ready, add to your pack a large supply of common sense, patience, and good humor, enough for the whole family, and a positive and enthusiastic attitude. Whatever happens, DON'T LOSE THESE! Your reward will be a lot of fun and many happy memories.

PART II

WHAT TO TAKE

Luxury or necessity? Over and over again, the backpacker of any age must ask himself that question. Should he take fishing gear and leave the air mattress at home? Or should he plan to sleep more comfortably and eat less well?

When the backpackers are parents who plan to take their children with them, the questions become even more crucial. Parents must be prepared to carry larger than normal loads, because they must carry some or all of their children's baggage. With small children the added *bulk* of special supplies can be as much of a problem as the extra weight in the pack. A baby on a hike requires diapers and other clothing, food, a few toys, clean-up materials for diaper changing, and perhaps sleeping gear. All these things, plus the child, are in addition to the parents' gear. Taking an older sibling means even more to carry.

How have other parents handled these difficulties? Let's consider each problem one at a time.

WHAT THE WELL-DRESSED HIKER WILL WEAR

Most people find that they already own adequate clothing to begin hiking. As they progress, they will want to add to their wardrobes items that can be useful for hiking and for other times too. This is true for children also; don't rush out to buy hiking clothes for your kids until you're sure they don't already own a garment that will work.

The important knowledge to be gained from a chapter on what to wear hiking is how to dress in such a way that you will be prepared for any conditions that you may run into. The weather can change quickly in the mountains or the desert. The season of the year makes a difference too; winter hikers must be prepared to give themselves much more protection than summer hikers. (However, hikers in the high country often experience freezing nights even in July and August.)

THE LAYERING SYSTEM

Hikers of any age and in any season should dress by a system called "layering," which allows them to add or subtract lightweight pieces of clothing as they adjust to weather conditions and their own body heat.

15

First, there is the underwear layer, soft material that controls moisture on the skin. Most people like to have their underwear somewhat loose in summer to allow some air circulation, but more snug in winter to retain heat. We used to say that this layer should be cotton or wool, to absorb perspiration and keep the skin from feeling clammy. Nowadays, there are man-made filaments that are completely non-absorbent; they act as wicks, to draw moisture away from the skin onto an outer absorbent layer. Polypropylene is the generic name of one of these fibers that is widely used. These fibers are knit into garments of differing weights and textures, suitable for varying temperatures and seasons. Depending on whether the hiker perspires a lot or not, whether he will be moving or still, and whether he likes the feel of the man-made fibers, he has a wide choice for the layer he wears next to his skin. In the summer, he may choose to wear just a cotton or polyester blend tee-shirt and underpants. In winter it would be wool or silk or fleece or polypropylene underwear, or a material that is double layers of wicking and absorbing materials. (I found underwear for kids in all these fibers in the Campmor catalogue. See Appendix B.) Some hikers who perspire a lot wear polypropylene underwear winter and summer.

Next in the layering system is an insulating layer; this insulation can be one warm garment or a combination of a shirt, sweater, sweatshirt, and a down vest, perhaps with warm pants in winter. Over this, the outer, protecting layer can be a parka, windbreaker, or similar wind-resistant garment. If this layer is not waterproof, then an additional layer—a poncho or a rain suit—is necessary. Layers can be added or removed one by one to adjust to changing temperatures. In winter a hiker may wear two sweaters under a parka; in summer he may not wear a second layer, but he would carry extra layers for warmth, wind, and rain protection in his pack. A child's snowsuit may serve as both the insulating and wind-resistant layers.

Adults and children who are walking will generate heat from the exercise; their needs are not the same as those of children who are being carried. Therefore, this chapter will consider first the needs of walking children, summer and then winter. Then we will take up the needs of non-walkers. Diapers and shoes, with their special problems, will be considered in separate sections.

SUMMER CLOTHING

Children should not need special clothing to wear hiking in good weather. Rather, their parents should select, from among the things they already have, the sturdiest and most comfortable garments, clothing that can keep them from overheating and that can be easily cared for.

Many parents who take their children hiking only in summer report that their family uniform is a lightweight long-sleeved shirt worn with long pants and a sun hat. This arrangement helps protect against sunburn, insect bites, stinging nettles, brush, and scrapes from falls. On very hot days, sleeves and pant legs can be rolled up, *although exposed arms and exposed legs will be unprotected*. Extra clothing carried in the pack—a sweater, a windbreaker, and rainwear—takes care of changes in the weather.

Most of the items in our summer wardrobes that we think of as cotton clothing are actually made of a blend of cotton with artificial fibers, like polyester, or even of 100% polyester. In hot weather, the blends are warmer and less absorbent than 100% cotton. Clothing made of the cooler, softer, all-cotton fabrics are sometimes difficult to find. The advantages of the artificial fibers are seen in the laundry room, not the woods; polyester dries more quickly and with fewer wrinkles than cotton. If you plan to wash some of your children's clothing on a hike, then perhaps a blend would be a better choice than an all-cotton fabric; but cotton is more comfortable.

Summer uniform—long sleeves, long pants, hat, and netting

Robert Judson

Whether an outfit is 100% cotton or a cotton blend, if it's all a child has when he's caught in a rainstorm, he's in trouble. Cotton and cotton blends are useless when you need garments that will hold body heat when wet; they cling to your skin and make you lose heat rapidly. That's why you should always carry extra clothing in your rucksack, to keep warm and dry or both.

The colors you choose for your children to wear on a hike can also affect their comfort. Dark colors absorb heat, so they make the wearer feel hotter; however, dark colors don't show dirt. Light colors show dirt more readily but are cooler because they reflect heat. Most backpackers expect to get dirty and therefore choose to be comfortable rather than to look clean.

Safety is another factor to consider when you choose the clothing that your child will wear on a hike. A bright red or yellow shirt will be easier to spot, if a child wanders off, than a green or a brown one.

The trousers that your child wears should be made of a sturdy, hard-finished material like denim, and should be loose enough to be comfortable and short enough that he won't trip over them. Lots of kids hike in jeans, but remember that jeans will feel uncomfortably cold when they are soaking wet. Some parents like pants with an elastic cuff, to keep bugs out. Sweatpants, made with an elastic cuff at the ankle, are a good choice if they're not too baggy. Some parents buy these pants oversize so the child can wear them longer; the elastic at the waist and ankles lets the child wear pants that are too big. If the pants are too loose, the baggy legs could interfere with the child's walking and snag on brush and rocks. Better dress him in old, short sweats for a hike.

When I wrote the first edition of this book, bell-bottom pants were the fashion. I warned parents that wide-legged or cuffed pants would catch on rocks or underbrush to trip the wearer, and that bell-bottoms were particularly dangerous around a campfire. Now I see kids in jeans with ragged hems that drag along the ground, and hope they're not going to wear them hiking. Stirrup pants with a strap that goes under the foot are less likely to trip up a child, so long as the pants aren't too tight for comfortable walking and the strap doesn't rub on the child's foot. (A fashion magazine has predicted that the next big news in fashionable women's pants will be bell bottoms again. If that is true, then little girls' bell bottoms will follow shortly, and the warning about not wearing them for camping bears repeating.)

Even on sunny days, when the family stops to rest the hikers begin to cool off. A slight breeze can penetrate a damp cotton shirt and start a child shivering. That's the time to haul out the windbreakers for everyone. When I grew tired of carrying jackets for all three children, I decided that this was one item that even the youngest, pack-less walker could manage for himself. At a yardage store I let each child pick a length of wide, decorative tape. I then sewed the tape to the inside of the children's jackets at three places: at the center of the back of the neck and on each side seam a few inches below the armhole. The tape was long enough to form two loops from the sides to the neck of the jacket. A child could put his arms through the loops and let the jacket hang down his back when not wearing it. Some children carry their own jackets by tying the sleeves around their waists. The loops are a little more secure, and they work for kids who can't tie.

Everyone who hikes should have a hat with a brim to protect his face, eyes, and neck. Inexpensive "tennis" hats can be purchased in most variety and department stores; Cathy's son wears his mother's old glacier hat that shrank in the wash. Or the

Straps to hold jacket; ski-pole walking stick

Don Silverman

hat can be made at home; many patterns are available. The brim of the hat should be sewn of two thicknesses of material: the upper cloth should be white to reflect the sun's rays and the lower material should be dark to absorb light reflected up off the ground or water. The hat should shade the back and sides of the child's neck. A square of mosquito netting pinned to the top of the hat can be draped over the child's shoulders to provide protection from insects. Don't let your child hike in the billed baseball cap that so many kids wear today, often backwards, unless he's willing to wear a bandanna draped to protect his ears and his neck from sun.

How much clothing should you pack for a child? Inexperienced hikers often try to take too much. Many adult backpackers wear the same pants and shirt for their entire trip. They believe that the extra weight and space in a pack can be put to better use carrying high-energy foods or protective layers of clothing rather than clean clothes, and they tolerate dirty and occasionally wet clothing.

This does not mean that parents should not take any spare clothes along for a child, but only that he doesn't need clean clothes every day. There are some emergencies that require dry, but not necessarily clean, clothing. Some families carry one complete change for each child, in case he falls in a creek, has a toileting accident, or gets soaked by rain. Another family carries one generic set of clothing for all the children; the first one who needs it, gets it. After that, they try to switch around garments to keep everyone comfortable. When nothing works any longer, they go home.

Experience warns, however, that parents should not be too hasty to change the child's clothes. If your daugh-

Some girls wear skirts, no matter what!

Goldie Silverman

ter is playing happily near a lake, wet to the knees, and you make her change her pants, in a short time the second pair will also be wet to the knees—or higher. Wait until the child is ready for the dry set of clothes and change her then.

Some parents may think that it is better to have too much clothing than too little. That may be true on a car trip to visit Grandma, but when you're backpacking, you will be carrying every ounce of the clean clothing. Kids seem to have a natural affinity for puddles, so take extra socks and perhaps one pair of extra pants. An extra fleece vest can be a great comfort on an extremely cold night. But a clean shirt every day? It's a lot easier to let your child wear the same shirt for four days. Turn it inside out if it really bothers you. At night when he takes it off, brush off the most obvious dirt and let it go at that.

SLEEPWEAR

Many adult backpackers crawl into their sleeping bags in the same clothes they wore all day—minus boots, of course. Some hikers strip down to their underwear layer to keep their sleeping bags somewhat clean. However, if the night is cold at all, clothes that are still slightly damp from a day of sweating will add to the chill. It is much wiser to change into a fresh clothes for sleeping. Let them air for a short while each morning and they will be warm and dry at bedtime. Children can follow the same procedure.

Good choices to take for children are warm, footed sleepers; long johns; or blanket sleepers. On cold nights a child will sleep in more layers, just as he wears more layers on cold days. Cathy carries sleepers that are "one season heavier" than the season of their hike. Judy puts double sleepers on her child. Hooded sweatshirts or fleece jackets are nice for extra warmth, or a child can wear a fleece hat and a sweater over his pajamas.

WINTER CLOTHING

A few years ago, the foul weather uniform for families that hike was definitely wool, which soaks up water slowly and provides warmth even when wet. The only alternative—down-lined clothing—was useless as insulation if it got wet, and it was too expensive for children's garments that were quickly outgrown. But wool fabrics were often itchy to wear, they required special laundering, and they smelled funny when wet—like a wet sheep!

Now there are lots of other choices in the marketplace. Non-woven fabrics of man-made fibers have been turned into garments that are sturdy, bright-colored, and inexpensive, as light-weight as the down-filled models and warmer than wool pound for pound when wet. If they are wrung out they will give up most of the moisture that is in them. They are wonderfully soft to the touch, they can be tossed into the washing machine and dryer, and they have no funny odor when wet. Look for fleeces and double-faced polyester pile under such brand names as Polartec®, Polarfleece® and Synchilla®. Fleece comes in varying weights, 100, 200, or 300, the larger the number, the greater the.warmth. Another plus: fleece is made from recycled plastic soda pop bottles. (My favorite brand is Polartec®, made by Malden Mills, because, after a huge fire destroyed the plant, the owner of the mill kept all his workers on the payroll while they were re-building.) Even a person not very skilled at sewing will find these fabrics wonderfully easy to work with; the edges of the cut fabric do not unravel, so the seams do not require special finishing. A good source for fabrics and patterns is Seattle Fabrics or the Malden Mills outlet stores (see Appendix B).

Some fleece fabrics are manufactured with a built-in windproof barrier, so that no additional windbreaker or parka is needed. Otherwise, your child will need something light to wear over his fleece jacket—a jacket or parka made of tightly woven fabric to keep the wind out, with a water-resistant coating to keep out rain. Again, clothing-makers are using a wide variety of bright-colored, light-weight, wind- and water-resistant fabrics. Some fabrics to look for include Supplex®, Berguntal Cloth®, Hydroseal®, Barrier Cloth®, and Chinook®. Another material is called simply "coated nylon." These fabrics are also found made into jackets or snow suits with light-weight interlinings that

Wool pants with suspenders and deep hems

have the same warmth and water-shedding qualities as fleece. Some of the brand names to look for in linings are PolarGuard®, Hollofil®, Quallofil® and Thinsulate®. (See catalogues listed in Appendix B.)

For more on the subject of waterproof outerwear, see the next section on Rainwear.

Not everyone loves fleece: some people prefer natural fibers over man-made. Those parents who still favor wool for their children's clothing have found it less easily available but not impossible to find. Wool or at least wool-blend underwear is still made for children. If you can't find it new, you can sometimes find it at ski-exchange sales, where parents try to replace outgrown skiwear with the next size up. With care, these garments can be passed down through several children. However, don't buy any ski pants at the sale even if they are wool; ski pants are generally too binding to be comfortable for hiking. Adult clothing that has been improperly laundered—sweaters or long underwear that have shrunk—can also be used for children.

Wool clothing for children may be difficult to find in stores, but it is very easy to make. A sale of remnants of washable wool at a yardage store can be a good, cheap source of material. Another good source is the Salvation Army or other salvage store. Military surplus stores also carry wool clothing; my winter hiking pants are Air Force blues. A pleated wool skirt or a man's suit could provide enough yardage for several pairs of children's pants; a loose vest for a child could be cut down from a woman's jacket. Hard-finished, tightly woven wool is the best choice for pants and jackets; the surface will not snag and it will provide some natural protection from rain. Use the soft, fuzzy, or nappy fabrics for linings and inner garments; for the best insulation, turn the fluffy side toward the skin.

Children in Europe, especially in the northern countries, are dressed in woolens much more commonly than American children. Some import shops that carry merchandise from Germany or the Scandinavian countries have wool pants. Travelers to Europe may find that wool clothing is a good gift to bring back to hiking families. European clothing is often cut with a much higher waistline than similar American garments, so our young hikers can wear them over many seasons. Five-year-old Terry has been hiking for two years in a pair of imported high-waisted wool trousers with deep hems at the ankles and elastic suspenders that will allow the pants to grow longer as Terry grows; his mother estimates he will get at least two more years' wear from them.

When children are dressed in appropriate layers for warmth, with an outside layer of some wind-and waterproof material, they can stay comfortable and happy even when the day is cold and wet. But extra care must be taken in choosing the layers that the child will wear. Some of the heavy, lined coats and padded jackets that many children wear to school every day are not good jackets to wear hiking. An hour's walking while wearing such a heavy garment may find the child soaked with perspiration. If he unzips the jacket, his heated body is exposed to chilling winds. He is much better off in a lighter-weight parka plus sweaters to add as needed.

Children who hike in areas that are cold and dry can combine their insulating layer and their wind-proof layer in one garment, such as a synthetic-filled parka. Hikers in wetter areas need to have reliable rainwear.

RAINWEAR

Some commercial children's rainwear is not suitable for the trail; it is made of stiff, heavy, rubberized material, or it fits too closely to allow for ventilation, or it does not cover the child adequately. Suitable rainwear is just the opposite: it is lightweight and folds to a compact bundle to fit into a pack; it covers the child completely, yet loosely enough to allow air to circulate and discourage condensation inside.

Children's rainwear—poncho or jacket and pants, made of nylon coated with urethane or other waterproofing—can be found in many outdoor and department stores. Look for clothing that has seams that were factory-sealed; otherwise, buy some sealer and do it yourself. After one season's wear, check the seams again; often the protection wears off.

Look at the placement of the seams; a jacket with a seam that runs from the neck across the shoulder and down the arm is much more likely to fail and soak the clothing inside than a jacket that has underarm seams. The hood should be one piece; a seam across the head might leak. After too many tragic accidents where children's drawstrings caught on swings or climbing bars, responsible clothing manufacturers no longer use drawstrings at children's necks or on their hoods; they use elastic or an arrangement of snaps or hook and loop fastening on tabs to keep the hood snug against the face. Better rainwear is often sewed with an extra layer in key spots; for example, a yoke across the shoulders is common. Rain pants with a long zipper down each leg are much easier to put on and take off over boots than those without zippers, but they are also more likely to leak through the zipper. Look for pants with a zipper or VELCRO® brand hook and loop fastener or elastic at the bottom to allow passage over the boot and then minimize the opening.

Recently, adult backpackers have turned in great numbers for their rain protection and other outdoor wear to fabrics laminated to a water-barrier membrane. This membrane is a

One-piece rainsuit, mittens on a string

Jeffrey Hancock

teflon-based film with microscopic holes that allow water vapor from perspiration to pass out, but prevent larger droplets of water, like raindrops, from penetrating. The membrane is bonded to an outer fabric, and sometimes it has a second, inner layer of lighter-weight fabric to protect it; in other words, the membrane is sandwiched between a cotton or nylon poplin on one side and nylon tricot on the other. The brand names for fabrics laminated this way include Gore-tex®, Entrant®, and Helly-Tech®. Campmor calls their product Camp-Tech. The brand refers to the film coating and not to the fabric. There may be other companies who have introduced similar products; look for the words, "waterproof breathable." When these products were first introduced they were much too expensive to be used in children's clothing that would soon be outgrown. Now as the fabrics have become more common, the price has dropped, and they are appearing more and more in children's clothing. Check the mail order catalogues in Appendix B for sources.

Good quality rainwear is an additional expense for the hiking family, and many parents choose to make their own. They use the same lightweight coated nylon that large manufacturers use, purchased by the yard. A poncho is simply a rectangle with a neck hole and a hood. It is supposed to be loose fitting, so it is a good project for an inexperienced clothing maker. If you can't find a pattern for a poncho, you may be able to find a pattern for a hood for some other garment, and adapt it to your poncho; just be sure that there is no seam down the center. Or use an adult's poncho for a model, and cut a smaller pattern to fit. Measure the child from one shoulder across the top of his head to the other shoulder to determine the size of the hood.

Fashion designers experiment with inexpensive muslin before they cut into costly fabrics. You can do the same. Make a poncho of newspaper or an old bedsheet before you try making it from your good material. (Check the neck hole, too; if you make it too small, you'll have to put a zipper or VELCRO® fastening in the front of the poncho.) Like other responsible clothing manufacturers, do not tighten the hood around the face with drawstrings that might end up around the child's neck; the hood should be held in place with snaps, elastic, or hook and loop fastening. Some manufacturers put the tightening device at the back of the hood.The sides of the poncho can be closed with VELCRO® brand fastening. If you make the poncho longer in the back than in the front, it will fit over a pack to keep it dry. But don't cut the poncho extra large with the idea that "he'll grow into it." He'll trip over it going uphill.

A parka for a child can be sewn from a pattern for a hooded jacket. Be sure to make it large enough to fit over his clothing and still allow air to circulate underneath; otherwise he'll gather condensation inside. A parka offers more protection from wind than a poncho does, but a poncho doesn't have as many problems with condensation. Which is the better choice? It depends on your child and the conditions you hike in. You decide.

To wear under the poncho or parka, make your child a pair of rain pants. The simplest kind are cut just like pajama bottoms with a drawstring at the waist. You can put elastic at the cuff if you like, to keep water out, or a zipper or VELCRO® fastening to make it easier to don and remove the pants while wearing boots.

Waterproof clothing must be sewed very carefully. Each thrust of the needle, each pin prick made during the laying out of the pattern, creates a tiny hole that may leak in the finished garment. The fewer holes that are made during construction, the less likely will there be leaks. For that reason, during the cutting-out process, the pattern should not be *pinned* on, but rather laid out and fastened with masking tape; if pins must be used, they should be placed in the seam allowance. Again, the garment should be designed so that seams lie in less crucial areas, like under the arm, rather than across the shoulders. Finally, each seam in the finished garment should be carefully sealed. Seam sealers are available either as liquids that are brushed on or as tapes that are pressed on.

If you can find waterproof, breathable material to make your rainwear, you will need to use special sewing techniques and special seam-sealing techniques that are not usually available to the home sewer. That's the reason, according to one manufacturer's representative, that such fabrics are sold to clothing manufacturers but not to yardage suppliers. When you do find these fabrics, possibly in a fabric outlet, be aware that the manufacturers might not stand behind the product if you have a bad result.

Parents who have been unable or unwilling to buy or to make children's rainwear have found ways of improvising protection from the weather. An old adult's poncho can be cut down to fit a child. A poncho intended for a bicycle rider adapts well to a smaller wearer. An adult-sized waterproof jacket makes a good child's raincoat; the sleeves should be cut down to size to avoid rolled-up cuffs full of water. If you adapt a garment that has a hood with a drawstring, remove the drawstring and invent some other way to pull the hood snugly around the child's face. Use elastic around the hood, snaps, ties that can't circle the neck, or VELCRO®-fastened bands. Some parents suggest using a plastic garbage bag with a hole for the face as emergency rainwear, but the potential dangers of teaching a child to put a plastic bag over his head seem to me to be so great that I would rather have my child soaked through before I would do that.

The same rainwear your child wears on winter hikes should go into his pack on summer trips.

COMPLAINTS ABOUT COLD

Some children complain a lot about cold feet when they hike. Children who have to spend a lot of time standing around will have colder feet than those who keep moving, but cold feet should not be a problem for an active child who is wearing warm fleece or wool-blend socks and a pair of sturdy boots (more about these later). Families who hike in soggy weather often carry extra socks to change into at mid-day, or when the socks they are wearing get wet.

For winter hiking, hats and mittens are absolute necessities. Here too fleece products will stay warm when wet, and they won't itch. Often a child who is complaining of cold feet will feel better after he puts on a hat. Old-timers knew this through experience; now there is a scientific explanation. About 25% of the blood coming from the heart goes to the head and neck, even though together they constitute only 10% of the total body surface. That's for an adult; the figures for a child are slightly different, depending on his size, but the message is the same: the head and the neck are radiating much more heat than the rest of the body. An unprotected neck or head is losing much body heat. A hooded jacket or a good hat and muffler will keep the heat in. Some parents put two hats on their child. Cathy dresses her son in a silk balaclava, which is soft and clinging, with a wool balaclava over it. This is especially nice for the child who complains that his wool hat is too itchy. When the temperature drops very low, a scarf loosely tied over the mouth and nose will keep the child's face warm and will also warm the air he is breathing.

Some children complain more of cold hands than of cold feet. Layering works for the hands too. Some hikers wear an inner glove of thin nylon or silk. Over that they wear a thick wool or fleece mitten, and over that a waterproof leather or Gore-tex® mitten. Children often wear just two layers, the thick mitten and the waterproof mitten. Some parents put adult-sized mittens over the child's mittens. Ski mittens and snowmobile mittens are often complete in themselves and need no inner lining. Marjorie didn't feel like paying the price for good waterproof mittens; she solved the problem by sewing mittens of polymer-coated nylon to wear over wool ones. Her mittens had a fancy inset thumb and elastic at the wrist, and she sealed the seams with sealing tape. A simpler mitten could be made of just two pieces of cloth cut from a pattern traced around the child's hand. Few parents try to get their small children's hands into gloves, but remember, for yourself, that mittens are always warmer than gloves.

Although waterproofing techniques are constantly being improved, many mittens are not as waterproof as their manufacturers claim. Leather mittens can be protected further with a waterproofing spray or goop applied a few days before they will be worn. Silicon-based sprays for waterproofing can be found in shoe-repair shops or with the shoe polishes in a hardware or sporting-goods store. Follow the directions on the package carefully. Pay special attention to the seams when you apply the waterproofing, and of course, *never* use such preparations on mittens that will be worn by a baby who still puts things in his mouth.

Even the best waterproofed mittens in the world won't do any good if they get lost or dropped into a puddle. Some parents carry an extra pair for each child, for emergencies. Others fasten the mittens to the jacket sleeves with old-fashioned elastic tabs and buckles; these handy gadgets are hard to find, but they

Mittens clipped on; mittens tied to a long ribbon

sometimes turn up in general stores or variety stores. You can also make a set using the buckles from an old pair of suspenders from a thrift shop. Or copy another old-fashioned idea and fasten each mitten to a long ribbon or braid of yarn that goes through the sleeves of the coat and across the back; that way the mittens are always attached to the coat.

CLOTHING FOR INFANTS AND TODDLERS

The child who is being carried in a baby carrier should be dressed by the layering system also. Many of the suggestions for the older child (e.g., using warm clothing in winter, wearing a long-sleeved shirt and a sun hat in summer) apply to the baby as well. Remember, though, that he is not moving and generating heat to keep himself warm, so on cold days he may need more layers than his parents.

A practical hiking outfit for an infant is a stretchy, one-piece knit or fleece playsuit; if it has feet, all the better. The suit designed with a long zipper that runs from the neck to one foot makes diaper changing much easier. Two or three playsuits can be worn at one time for better insulation. In your grandparents' day (and in parts of Europe today) babies were routinely dressed in hand-knit or crocheted wool pants, jacket, and hat. Such outfits can still be found at church bazaars or senior citizens' craft shops, often knit of washable man-made yarns. Creative parents could whip up a three-piece suit while the baby naps. Or maybe a willing grandmother could knit a suit, or a traveling friend could bring one back. The pants alone, crocheted in a loose stitch, would work as infant long johns.

Many parents like to have one set of clothes for their infant for each day of an extended trip. Infants' clothing tends to collect an odor of urine that makes it unwearable a second time without a good washing. Changing the baby more than once a day is a nuisance, but most parents carry an extra suit or two in case a diaper cover leaks. A second or third suit worn over other clothing for insulation can usually be used on more than one day. If a baby spits up a lot, parents should carry bibs.

An older child, a toddler who walks part of the time and rides in a carrier part of the time, can wear the same sturdy overalls or crawlers that he wears at home, with a warm sweater, jacket, hat, and mittens. Since trouser legs tend to ride up in the carrier, the child's legs need extra protection. Tights worn under the overalls will provide an additional layer of insulation. Some parents dress their youngsters in knee-high socks for hiking trips. Anita knitted toddler-sized leg warmers, wool tubes the length of the child's leg, that rolled up over his pant legs. David improvised long johns by putting his daughter's legs through the sleeves of his own polypropylene underwear shirt and pulling the body of the shirt up under her arms. A pair of adult's wool socks can be pulled on right over the child's shoes and pants up to the knees to keep his legs warm; pin them in place with two safety pins to keep them from sliding down or getting lost. The Tarmegan company (see Appendix B) makes Rosie Tosies, tall fleece socks designed to pull up over their matching fleece pants; VELCRO® fastened straps keep the Tosies in place. Of course some of these garments would have to be removed when the child is taken out of the carrier to walk.

Mittens should also be fastened to the child, as described above.

A nylon windbreaker is a good outer layer for a young child on a mild day. If your infant doesn't have one, wrap an adult's jacket around him. In colder weather, he needs a snowsuit. Some very practical one-piece models are available, through catalogues if not in your local shops, which start out with a bag bottom that converts into legs with buttoned-on bootees. When the child begins to walk, the bootees can be removed, but if he rides in a carrier part of the time, the bootees will keep his feet warm and keep his pant legs from riding up. One mother whose baby was not yet walking simply sewed shut the cuffs on the legs of his snowsuit, so she wouldn't have to bother with pulling them down all the time. If the snowsuit has button-on mittens and a hood, it will completely windproof the baby. If the hat is separate, a muffler around the neck will prevent heat loss.

You may want to choose a two-piece snowsuit for your toddler. Then the jacket can be worn separately in mild weather. The toddler's snowsuit should not be so baggy that the child can't walk. One mother made a down-filled snowsuit for her daughter to wear hiking. She made it extra long so it would still cover the child even if it rode up on her legs in the carrier. But when the little girl tried to walk, the snowsuit was too long. For one whole season, the parents had to tie a belt or scarf around the girl's waist to hold up the snowsuit when she wanted to walk. By the next winter, she had outgrown the baby carrier, the snowsuit fit just right, and the child could walk beltless.

Parents who try to carry their snowsuit-clad children in their arms for even a short distance should consider the appropriateness of their own clothing. A father wearing a nylon jacket tried to carry his son who was wearing a nylon snowsuit. With no friction between the two bodies, nylon against nylon, he had a hard time keeping the child from sliding to the ground.

On a mild day, a hat that ties or buttons under the chin will keep the baby's head and ears warm. There should be a brim on the hat to protect the baby's eyes from sunlight from above; however, he may still be bothered by glare from below or the sun reflecting off the bright metal of his carrier. Some parents wear dark, dull colors themselves to reduce glare into the child's face. Others wrap the bright metal parts of the baby carrier with black tape or a kerchief.

When night falls and the infant or toddler is ready for bed, what then? Toddlers can sleep in the same footed pajamas and blanket sleepers that they wear at home. Infants can wear the same kind of knit playsuit at night that they wear during the day. Putting a fresh playsuit on the infant keeps him warmer and dryer all through the night. Next day he wears the playsuit until bedtime.

RAINWEAR FOR INFANTS AND TODDLERS

When it rains, many parents of infants and toddlers in dryer parts of the country simply call the whole trip off, either because they don't like to expose their children to bad weather or because their kids are pretty unbearable when it rains. In the Northwest, where I live, hikers would never get out if they allowed rain to deter them; babies here go out in all kinds of weather. Until recently, there was very little rainwear available. A large manufacturer tried to market a tiny poncho to fit over a baby in their soft front carrier, but discontinued it when it didn't sell well; however, some smaller companies have begun to develop new designs. In the Babyworks catalogue, I found Snookums®, a waterproof, loose-fitting rain poncho, in sizes 6 months to 4 years. It will fit over a child riding in a baby carrier. Tough Traveler® makes the Caper, a poncho that fits over a child riding in any of their carriers, and the Macaw, a heavier fleece-lined water-repellent cover; it has a top cape-like cover and a bottom bag-like cover. At a recent TrailsFest in Seattle, I met Tim and Megan Ratcliffe, who have started a company called Tarmegan. They make Puddle Stompin™ Raingear, bright-colored jackets, ponchos, and pants in small sizes, and a one-piece rain suit that is infant-size! Tarmegan rainwear is lightweight, simple, compressible, and waterproof, and the makers claim that it is cut large enough to fit a child through two years. See Appendix B for information on finding these products, or ask around locally to see if anyone in your area is making similar articles.

In the old days, parents who wanted rainwear for their babies had to learn to make do or make their own. These are projects for people who like to sew and who are not afraid to experiment with scissors and no pattern. Here again a newspaper or old bedsheet can be used to make a preliminary model.

Home-made two-headed poncho

Some experiments don't work. An adequate poncho for a child who is riding in a soft carrier in front of his parent would be nearly impossible to make. Though the baby's head and back could be protected, water from the parent's clothing would saturate the carrier and its straps, and eventually soak the child. A better idea for a parent who needs to carry an infant in a front carrier through the rain is to wear a waterproof parka or poncho large enough to cover the carrier with the child inside.

A two-headed poncho of waterproof cloth can be constructed for a baby who is being carried on a parent's back. The small head is about three-quarters the size of the large head, and is made just like it. Allow ten inches of material between the back of the large hood and the front of the small one. If the distance is too short, the child will be pulled forward, and if it's too long, the fabric between the hoods will sag and collect water. The small hood must have a lip at the bottom of the opening, or else water will run in. The poncho can be used by an adult alone if VEL-CRO® fastened tabs and a flap are added to hold the second hood out of the way and covered.

A separate baby's poncho can also be sewn for the child in a backpack carrier. Both the parent and the baby then wear ponchos when it rains. The child's poncho must be designed to cover the entire carrier; otherwise the carrier will fill with water. A tiny pair of rain pants made of the same waterproof material will keep the child's legs from being soaked by water draining off the parent's poncho. The pants should cover the child's feet.

Another option for the small child riding in a backpack is a one-piece hooded rainsuit of waterproof material that is created from a pattern for a snowsuit. The rainsuit should be large enough to wear over warm clothing, and the zippers should be protected by flaps to prevent leaking.

The seams of any garment that is intended for rainwear should be sealed, of course, and a child riding in a carrier in the rain should be checked often to be sure his rain protection has not failed.

THE CHANGING SCENE — DIAPERS

The Indian papoose rode happily in a cradleboard with a nest of dry moss to collect urine and feces. Tibetans used a handful of yak hair for the same purpose. Babies on a backpack trip cannot be handled so easily. In the absence of yak hair, modern babies wear diapers, which present two problems: bulky diapers must be carried in; used diapers must be carried out.

CHOOSING DIAPERS

Parents today choose between two types of diapers, cloth or disposable.

Flat-fold cloth diapers are a single thickness of either gauze, flannel, or birdseye cotton material in a square or oblong shape which requires folding, so that when the child wears the diaper, the greatest thickness will be in the center. A prefolded diaper of similar materials comes with the thickest section stitched in the center. Some prefolds have an inner lining that makes them more absorbent. Most cloth diapers need to be pinned around the baby, but the Baby Bunz & Co. and Babyworks (see Appendix B) carry shaped, pre-folded cloth diapers that fasten with VELCRO® brand hook and loop fasteners.

A separate waterproof pant worn over cloth diapers prevents urine from soaking into the child's clothing. Many baby stores carry plastic pants to pull over pinned diapers, but if you search hard enough for an outlet of special baby products, you can find waterproof covers made of cotton or wool where the diaper isn't pinned; it's folded and laid on the cover, which fastens around the baby with VELCRO® brand fastener. Baby Bunz and Babyworks both carry a model from Japan called a *Nikky*, which comes in all-cotton and breathable-poly models. These two mail-order houses also carry diaper covers made of waterproof nylon and wool felt, and they both have thick cotton pads to lay on a diaper to double its absorbency without adding bulk around the legs.

Flat-fold diapers may be hard to find; Gerber Baby Products (see Appendix B) manufactures both flat and prefolded.

Disposable diapers come in many styles and sizes, but most of them consist of three layers. The outer layer is waterproof and makes an additional pant unnecessary. The middle layer is an absorbent material; some brands contain a crystal that turns to a gel when it comes in contact with urine. The inner layer touches the skin and wicks moisture away to the middle layer. The latest designs feature elastic at the leg; super-absorbency at strategic places for girls or boys; and adhesive tabs at the waist to adjust to the baby's size, prevent leakage, and make diaper pins unnecessary.

A second kind of disposable is just the super-absorbent material in a thick pad, something like a sanitary napkin, that is placed inside of a standard diaper, either cloth or disposable, to double its absorbency. One brand is called Diaper Doublers.

A third type of disposable is the thin liner meant to be worn inside a cloth diaper to collect feces and keep the cloth diaper unstained. Gerber makes these too; they're called E Z Liners.

For the backpacking parent, there are the advantages and disadvantages to each type. Whatever method you decide is right, be sure to carry more diapers than you think you will need. If the baby isn't changed frequently enough, her clothing and her carrier might get soaked, creating all sorts of new problems.

**Hanging diapers
in the sun**

Goldie Silverman

CLOTH DIAPERS

C loth diapers are cheaper in the long run, especially if you launder them at home, and they are a re-usable resource, an important factor to anyone concerned with preserving forests. How many millions of trees have been felled to provide the materials for disposable diapers? Clean cloth diapers can be wadded up into a tight little mass and stuck into all sorts of odd spaces in a pack. They can also be used as bibs, towels, or wash cloths. Some people believe that cloth diapers are less irritating than disposables. Their disadvantage? They must be taken home and washed, or, on long trips, washed in camp.

Diapers that will be washed in camp must be the flat fold kind; thicker prefolded diapers take too long to dry. Stevie's family carries a two-day supply of diapers for her, one dozen diapers per day plus two extra. When they think Stevie is likely to poop, they line her diaper with a paper liner, and either bury it or drop it into a pit toilet if there is one at their campsite. They carry a plastic wash basin to wash diapers in. The basin fits into a pack with other supplies inside and around it. They say that it actually takes up very little room, and the family also uses it for washing the other children and the dishes. Every night, they wash the diapers in biodegradable soap, twist them as hard as they can to get every bit of water out, and hang them up under their rainfly.

Other parents reject the idea of washing diapers. First of all, there are the additional weight and mass of the extra fuel for heating water and the necessity for carrying the wash basin. (You would certainly not wash diapers in a stream.) Next there is the unpleasant task of washing diapers by hand. You must scrub the diapers in hot soapy water and then rinse them at least twice to remove irritating soap residue. Waste water should be dumped where it won't pollute, at least one hundred feet away from any lake or stream. The wet diapers must then be hung to dry on a clothesline or spread on bushes in the sun, or under a rainfly at night. Some people object to the sight of a dozen diapers strung on a line, as contrary to their idea of a wilderness experience. Stevie's parents claim that her diapers dry overnight even on wet nights, but then admit that they are sometimes just a tad damp the next morning. An unexpected two days of rain could spell disaster to a family that was counting on washing diapers.

Some parents who use cloth diapers take a large enough supply to last the whole trip and carry the used ones out in a strong double plastic bag tied to the outside of a pack. Some people wrap each diaper, or each day's diapers, in a separate plastic bag that goes into the larger bag; they say it helps keep the odor down. Others recommend spreading each day's diapers on the ground in the sun as soon as you reach camp, to dry them out a bit and reduce their weight; then wrap them in the plastic bags.

Other parents purchase "retired" cloth diapers from a diaper service to take hiking. These diapers are sanitary and absorbent, yet cheap enough to be dumped in the garbage can at home. The Yellow Pages of the telephone book is a good place to look for potential suppliers.

DISPOSABLE DIAPERS

Disposable diapers are efficient and fast; they are diaper and plastic pant combined, and they require the least amount of handling. However, disposables are expensive, more than twice as expensive as cloth diapers washed at home. Clean disposable diapers tear more readily than cloth ones, so they cannot be wadded up and stuck in a pack. But the biggest problem with so-called disposable diapers is that they are not really disposable at all. The plastic layer that covers them is a special insult to the environment, since it never decomposes but remains plastic litter forever. (I've heard the arguments that in communities where water is scarce or where waste is burned to provide power, disposable diapers are less insulting to the environment than cloth ones; perhaps this is true, but far more diapers are going into landfills than into incinerators, and we don't really know what harm might be coming to our atmosphere from the burning plastic and super-absorbent crystals.)

Even so-called biodegradable diapers will not degrade when they are buried deep in a landfill. The Bureau of Applied Research in the Department of Anthropology of the University of Arizona in Tucson has a research program called the Garbage Project. Beginning in the mid-'80s, these researchers have dug up 16 landfills in different parts of the country. I talked to a research associate, Timothy Jones, about their findings. He told me that no one had really studied the contents of landfills before they began the Garbage Project. Designers of landfills assumed that organic materials would compost, that biodegradable materials would decompose, and that enough methane gas would be generated to be used for power. None of this is happening. Deep in the oldest landfills, they found forty-year-old (1953) newspapers that were still legible. They found composting and methane gas in the top two or three feet of newer fills, where oxygen was still available, but as the landfills aged and as the oxygen was used up, these processes ceased.

Despite my fascination with the Garbage Project, I know I probably haven't dissuaded many people from carrying disposable diapers into the wilderness, so let's consider what to do with them. The easiest method of taking care of used disposable diapers and the way that is least harmful to the environment is to PACK THEM ALL OUT. Plastic covered diapers should be carefully folded in upon themselves so the plastic contains the moisture. Or, like cloth diapers, disposables can be wrapped in small plastic bags or spread in the sun to dry out before being packed.

Parents who have tried to dispose of diapers in camp report so many limitations on their methods that it's impossible to recommend any, but for the record, this is what they have tried.

Burning is the first option that most people think of. Unfortunately, parents can't stop to burn a diaper every time they change the baby, so they still must have some means of transporting used diapers. A wet diaper does not burn readily; a bag of wet diapers burns even more poorly. Some parents say they try to spread the diapers to dry first and then burn them.

The plastic layers, and possibly the absorbent middle layers, release harmful vapors when they are burned. Some parents rip the plastic cover off the diaper to carry out with the garbage; they burn just the inner layer. But all agree that it takes a very hot fire to get a diaper to burn. Current wilderness ethics discourage hikers from building big campfires, and in fact many areas forbid any fires at all. Where small fires are allowed, some people find it distasteful to burn diapers in their cooking fire. One family burns diapers only when they make beach hikes and have big fires of driftwood, but in many areas driftwood fires are not allowed, and even where they are, many responsible campers choose not to build them. Better to find a different way.

Burying the used disposable diaper is the second thing people think of to try to get rid of it. When the middle layer of the disposable diaper was made of absorbent fibers, people figured it would break down eventually, so they buried it in their toileting area with their other wastes. The plastic cover will not degrade, so it went into the garbage bag. But here again, burying is no longer acceptable to many outdoors people for a variety of reasons; it attacks the environment and it attracts animals. A toilet trench that will include buried diapers will have to be much larger than a trench that is prepared just for the usual body wastes. And now that there are super-absorbent crystals in the middle layer, we can no longer expect that material to break down.

In some popular wilderness areas, there are pit toilets to take care of the problem of large amounts of human wastes. Some people dump their disposable diapers here. There's nothing really wrong with doing this so long as you drop in just a liner or the inner layer and not the plastic cover. Keep in mind, however, that the faster the pit is filled, the sooner a new one will have to be dug, making another scar on the landscape.

CHANGING DIAPERS

Along with more than enough diapers, parents should also be sure that they have adequate supplies for clean-ups at changing time. The Coopers, out on a dry trail, discovered they had cotton balls and paper tissues for wiping the baby, but they had forgotten to bring a plastic bottle of water or lotion. The only liquid they had was a little can of apple juice, so for a few hours they had a sweet-smelling, clean, but sticky baby.

In any drugstore you can find a number of brands of wipers—tissues soaked with oil or lotion—intended for diaper-changing times. Some of them come in pop-up containers and some of them are labeled "biodegradable." That doesn't mean you can leave the wipers behind; you should still pack them out. If you transfer the wipes from their hard-sided container to a plastic bag with a zipper closing, you make more room in your pack. Another wipe that can be used for diaper clean-ups is the kind made for adult vaginal or anal cleansing; these are often packed in individual foil packets. Before you take any package of wipers on an outing, check to be sure that the lotion won't leak out of the container, that the tissue is not so small that it's useless, and that the lotion doesn't irritate your baby's skin.

After the baby has been changed, the person who did the job will need something to clean his own hands. Premoistened hand or face towels in foil packets work well here and are easy to carry with the baby's things; however, there is an important precaution to remember. Some premoistened towels contain alcohol, which can be very painful to tender or irritated skin. Never use these hand towels on the baby's bottom.

The foil packages that wipers are wrapped in should be carried out with the litter; otherwise they will remain forever as part of the landscape. The wipers themselves are designed to stay moist for a long,

A comfortable place for changing

Don Silverman

long time without disintegrating, and therefore they do not degrade as easily as other kinds of paper. Alcohol dries very quickly in air, so when you finish with the hand towels, stuff them in your pocket, and leave them there until you need either some cloths that can be moistened without falling apart or a fire starter. They work excellently either way.

IF THE SHOE FITS, WEAR IT

Good shoes for children are important. Not only do they make hiking more fun for the child, but they make hiking safer too. A child without good foot support will spend much time complaining, or asking to be carried. On the other hand, hiking boots for children are expensive and are soon outgrown. How do hiking families solve this problem?

FINDING BOOTS

Just as adult clothing styles come and go, so too styles in children's clothing are cyclical. A few years ago, "patrol boots"—ankle-high, smooth, tan leather boots with ripple soles—and "waffle stompers"—rough leather shoes with lug soles—were the style for children to wear every day, and that's what they wore hiking too. Both were sturdy shoes with good tread and good ankle support, they could be found in every department store, and they could be waterproofed. If you're lucky, you might find a used pair for your child in a thrift shop or at a garage sale even now.

In the late '90s, similar shoes have appeared. They are high-tops made of heavy-duty leather and with good arch support; the manager of the children's shoe department at Nordstrom calls them "street hikers." These shoes have the look of a boot, but

44

not the built-in features of a technical hiking boot. Nevertheless, they would work well for dayhiking and short overnight trips.

Another style for children's everyday shoes that is seen often on the trail is some variation of the athletic shoe, the sneaker or tennie runner, a cloth or leather laced shoe with a rubber sole. Some athletic shoes can be found in high-top styles, and some have patterned soles designed to grip the walking surface. In good weather, on a dry trail, any of these styles is an adequate shoe; many parents report that their children have had no problems hiking in sneakers. My consultant at Nordstrom warned that canvas shoes, even the high-tops, do not offer much support; leather shoes are much better. There is a temptation to save the kids' newest shoes for school and send them hiking in their older pairs, but as athletic shoes age, the tread on the soles tends to disappear. Then the smooth rubber soles are very slippery on wet logs and rocks, and on snow or ice, and the shoes are not safe to wear hiking.

If children will be hiking in cold or rainy weather, or if parents want better ankle support, athletic shoes won't do. Then parents must look beyond their department stores, and even beyond most outdoors stores, to find real hiking shoes for children.

Stiffer, high-top hiking boots with good lug soles can be found in children's sizes but it takes some searching. If there are no shoes available in your area, the Campmor and the L.L. Bean catalogues (see Appendix B) offer several styles. The Nordstrom store in Seattle doesn't have a catalogue, but they will accept mail or telephone orders. If Nordstrom doesn't have the kind of shoes that you want in stock, their staff will search through catalogues to find and special-order them for you. You can call Nordstrom collect to discuss your needs: (206) 628-2111; the children's shoe department extension is 1460. Ask for the manager or someone who has been in children's shoes for a few years. She will tell you how to make a tracing of your child's feet so they can send the proper size. Campmor guarantees unused merchandise for up to one year of purchase; L.L.Bean promises 100% satisfaction. Still, ordering shoes by mail is risky; allow plenty of time before your planned hike in case you have to exchange the first pair that arrives.

Fit is the most important factor when choosing children's—or anyone's—shoes. When the child is fitted for boots, slide the child's foot forward as far as possible and stick one finger down the back of the heel. If one finger fits snugly and the child can still wiggle her toes a bit, the fit is good. Flexibility is important too; shoes should be stiff enough to give support but not so stiff that they impede the child's walking. An experienced salesperson can give you the best advice, based on your child's age, weight, walk and so on. Be sure to try boots on with the sock combination that the child will wear while hiking. Let your child walk around indoors wearing the boots; Nordstrom will exchange shoes that have not been worn outdoors.

After parents invest in hiking boots for their children, they want them to be wearable as long as possible. However, don't buy shoes that are too big with the idea that your child can wear them over heavier socks the first season, and thin socks the next. Walking in shoes that are too big is uncomfortable and dangerous. Find some other way of beating the high cost of children's boots. Boots are unisex; it's possible to pass them down through several children. Many families share outgrown boots with other families. One advantage of joining a hiking club is to

**Simple,
serviceable shoes**

Don Silverman

find families whose children may be a size larger or smaller than yours. Or you can use a hiker's newsletter to buy or sell usable outgrown footwear.

For winter hiking, many parents choose rubber boots with heavy felt liners worn over several pairs of socks. One mother suggests getting over-the-shoe rubber boots to wear with shoes one year, and with heavy socks the second.

Some experienced hikers carry an old pair of athletic shoes or a pair of lightweight vinyl rubbers on an extended hike; they put these on, sockless, to wade streams. (You sometimes see the wet shoes hanging on the outside of their pack to dry.) Some hikers like to wear these softer shoes in camp, to give their boots and their feet a rest. You and your children could follow that example. If your hike ends near a shallow lake or stream, wading in these extra shoes could be a fun activity for your child. However, if everyone in the family wants a second pair of shoes, a parent might end up carrying an unreasonable number of shoes. Extra shoes might be one of the items in a child's first pack.

Children need to break in new boots gradually, just as adults do. After you have set up your preferred arrangement of shoes and socks, let them wear their boots around the neighborhood before taking a hike in them.

SOCKS

The arrangement of socks most hikers prefer is one pair of heavy knit socks over one pair of thin inner socks. The inner sock should act as a wick to draw perspiration away from the skin to the absorbent heavy sock. The inner sock is also supposed to fit snugly, like a second skin, so that the friction of walking is between the two socks, rather than from sock sliding on skin. These days the inner sock is usually made of silk or of some synthetic material designed for superior wicking. The outer sock is probably a wool-synthetic blend, but it could be fleece. A problem with this arrangement is that a wrinkle can form in the sock material, leading to a blister. To avoid blisters, some companies make a product that combines the two functions in one sock.

Children can wear the same arrangement of socks. For outer socks, wool-blend or synthetic socks are preferred by most parents for their children, because they retain their shape better than cotton socks do, and that helps to prevent blisters. Knee-high socks stay up better in children's boots than socks of ankle height.

A tube sock, one that is knit without a heel, is an excellent sock for kids. No matter how the child pulls it on, it fits. Some outdoor stores sell tube socks for children; a knitter of modest skill could easily make a pair. Simply cast on to three needles as many stitches as you need. Use the child's leg as a guide; the number of stitches will vary with the yarn, the needles and the child. Knit-purl a cuff of desired length, and then knit the sock to length. Bind off the end just as you would for the toe of any sock or for a mitten.

Some children's feet are tougher than adults' and can take abuse with no problems. Other kids are real "tender feet." Their parents must keep constant watch so the socks don't slide down in their shoes and cause instant blisters. A wrinkle in a sock or a lump of threads can be a villain. Listen to the child who complains about his feet, and apply moleskin at the first sign of redness or a hot spot.

Since most children seem to operate on the theory that the way to get past a puddle is to plod straight through, it's wise to pack extra socks, even on a dayhike.

If you can't find kids' socks in the stores near your home, look in the catalogues in Appendix B.

PACKS TO CARRY KIDS,
PACKS FOR KIDS TO CARRY

Parents soon learn that the farther you carry a child, the heavier she becomes. It would be impossible to take a child, a non-walker, on a hike without some kind of device for carrying her. A babe in arms may feel warm and safe, but the arms soon feel numb and stiff. A child riding on an adult's shoulders might forget to hold on; she is unprotected if the adult falls; and she is likely to be hit in the face by branches or brush.

Baby-carrying devices have become very popular in recent years. Parents who decide to invest in one will find that there is a wide variety available, and numerous places where they are sold. "Invest" is not a word chosen lightly; shoppers will find a broad range of styles and prices, with some models in the luxury class. Backpacking stores are not the only places to look for carriers; children's stores, department stores, variety stores, and hardware stores all sell them. The catalogues of large mail-order houses are likely to show several styles of baby carriers. At garage sales or consignment shops, you may find used ones. It is possible to buy a carrier with all sorts of devices to make carrying easier, but there are still parents with limited budgets and others who enjoy devising their own equipment who are creatively developing their own products.

CRADLEBOARD

A carrier for an infant must support her neck and head. The American Indians used a cradleboard for this. Anyone can make one. First cut a board of some strong but lightweight material to shape; quarter-inch-thick plywood or half-inch Styrofoam would make a good base. Experiment with newspaper patterns to get the size just right. A little shelf of the material sticking out at a right angle provides something for the baby to "stand" on. Then cover the cradleboard with padding and fabric. Extend the fabric over the baby on either side so it can be laced together. If the lacing comes down from the top, the baby's diapers can be changed easily without removing her from the cradleboard. The cradleboard is held on the parent's back by a set of straps that go from the top of the board over the parent's shoulders and back to the board. Test the straps in different

Cradleboard

Jeff Berman

places to find the most comfortable way to wear them. A shade frame attached to the top of the cradleboard can hold netting or a diaper to keep insects and sun off the baby's face. Some makers suggest adding underarm straps to help hold the baby in position. Otherwise, a newborn will slide down into the wrappings; her head will be barely visible above the top edge. But an infant of three to four months will be held securely upright, able to gaze around.

SOFT CARRIERS AND SLINGS

A good investment for young parents, one that can be used from newborn to toddler stage, is the very popular soft pack. These used to be corduroy or denim sacks that held the baby spread-eagled across her parent's chest. We tended to call them all "snugglies," but this term should be reserved for the Snugli® brand carrier, which was the original pack. Now the soft carrier is less enveloping, and it comes with a firm back support. Snugli® brand carriers can still be found through the Evenflo Company, which now owns the Gerry® and Snugli® lines. (See Appendix B.) When you shop for a soft pack, look for an inner seat that adjusts to accommodate the growing child, a padded harness for the baby, padded straps for the parent, and a strap for a pacifier or a toy. On some models, there are two carrying positions, face-in or face-out, and on some, the pack can be reversed and worn on the back.

A sling is another kind of carrier that works quite nicely for a baby up to the age of four months or so. Small babies seem to like to be carried in slings. The baby is close to her parent and receives a minimum of jiggling. One type of sling on the market holds the baby across the parent's chest, with the baby's head nestled in the crook of the parent's arm. Another holds the baby on the parent's side, on one hip.

Sling devices can easily be made at home. One way to start is by sewing a pair of short pants for the baby out of sturdy cloth, such as denim. (You can use the legs saved from a pair of jeans when you make cut-offs.) The pants must be large enough to fit over the baby's other clothing and come up under her arms. If the child's head still needs support, the pants should come up higher in back so that a panel goes over her head. Wide straps from the

Michael Boguch

Mother with child wrapped in Komori-band

back of the pants go up over the parent's shoulders. Another two straps start at the side seams of the pants and go around the parent's chest. The four straps meet on the parent's back with buckles, ties or D-rings, whatever the maker finds easiest to use and most comfortable to wear. This sling can be worn on the back also.

Another sling that can be made at home consists of a simple rectangle of denim with a ring at each of the lower corners. The rectangle passes between the baby's legs to form a kind of seat. Long ties from the upper two corners of the rectangle go under the baby's arms and over the parent's shoulders; they criss-cross the back (or the chest, if the baby rides on the back) and come around the body to tie onto the metal rings. A roll of foam rubber covered by the denim fabric at each end of the rectangle will help to hold the baby in place.

If the sling or soft pack is worn on the parent's chest, it is possible to carry an additional load in a backpack.

In the Baby Bunz & Co. catalogue, I found the Baby Bundler™, a stretchy cotton wrap that can hold a baby in a variety of positions. The bundler comes with both written instructions and a video.

A somewhat similar device is the Japanese Komori-band, which translates as "care-for-child-band." It consists of a piece of strong cotton approximately 10 inches wide and 12½ feet long which must be artfully wrapped around parent and child. You can make the band yourself, find one at a Japanese import store, or ask a traveler going to Japan to bring one back..

To begin the complex envelopment, the child leans against her parent's back as if to begin a piggyback ride. The parent centers the strip of cloth on the child's back at the mid-chest level, then brings the ends under the child's arms and over the parent's shoulders. The parent then crosses the band over her chest and brings the ends around in back of her and the child to cover and support the child's hips and bottom. Each end continues around to be tied securely over the parent's abdomen.

Parents who have used this Komori-band claim that it is comfortable on a long hike for both parent and child, and that even a three-year-old can be carried this way. In addition, it folds up easily to be tucked away when the child is walking.

A Nigerian child-care professional has adapted a traditional African cloth carrier for American convenience and safety. She calls it Baby Wrap; it is a strapless, denim wrap that goes on very quickly. (See Appendix B.)

Many other cultures use similar systems of carrying infants by wrapping them in cloth or other materials; you may wish to investigate further to see if one of these methods would work for you.

A good pack takes a lot of thought and research, but would you believe a soft pack could have been the subject of a master's thesis? When Cathy Jeffris earned the degree of Master of Science in Home Economics and Family Studies from Central Washington University in Ellensburg, Washington, she designed a pattern for a soft pack. Cathy studied available packs first before she developed her own. Her pack has adjustable crossed straps, a waist belt, and readily available hardware. It is easy to put on, inexpensive to make, washable, and compact enough to fold into a pocket. If you would like to see Cathy's pattern, ask your librarian to get you a copy of the thesis through inter-library loan (see Appendix C for full title).

One of my resources, Roger, reported that they never bothered with fancy slings; he carried his newborn swinging in an adult's shirt, with the sleeves tied around his neck. He must have wrapped the tails of the shirt around the baby somehow. This is not recommended for everyone!

BACKPACK CARRIER

As soon as the baby can hold her head up steadily, she can be put into a backpack carrier that consists of a canvas or nylon seat slung from a metal frame. A stiff magazine, a

**Backpack carrier
with strut**

Goldie Silverman

piece of shaped polyurethane foam, or a flat pillow can be insert-
ed into the back of the carrier to help support the baby, or blankets and diapers can be padded around her for support. In cold
weather, choose items for this space that will provide extra
warmth and insulation for the baby. Sweaters, clothing, a sleeping bag liner—any of these things stuffed into the carrier will
help insulate the baby from the cold air. In hot weather, the baby
will need to be supported but will also need to have air circulat-
ing around her. A pad for the front of the carrier will provide a
soft resting spot for the baby's head, or a folded sweater or other
garment can be used.

     Child carrier packs now come in several designs with a
number of options. Most packs let the child face forward, where
she is within a hair tug of Dad or Mom. Conversation is easier
this way, and the child can see the person carrying her, which
seems to make some children happier. Luxurious new designs
feature high back rests, padded sides, and padded safety straps
for the baby, carefully engineered hip and shoulder suspensions
for the parent, and zippered storage compartments underneath.
Look for such features as a seat that can be removed from the
frame for easy washing, an optional sun and rain hood, and a net

that fits over pack and child. There should be plenty of leg room for your child, and the seat should be adjustable so the pack grows with her. Tough Traveler® makes stirrups for the larger child whose feet hang below the packframe, and extra bags and pockets that can be attached to the carrier. You have to decide among these options which are most important to you; they are not inexpensive.

The less expensive carrier, the simple fabric seat slung from a metal frame, is also still around, but now it comes with a padded headrest. Evenflo makes a carrier with wheels that converts to a stroller. Most carriers have an extra metal bar that swings out so the pack can stand alone as a seat; this pack can be very convenient for feeding the baby in camp or letting her sit up and watch her parents set up a tent or cook dinner. In a garage sale or other source of used equipment, you may find an older model that allowed the child to sit facing backwards if she wished to; some parents prefer to carry the child this way. There is less likelihood that the child will be hit in the face with branches and brush; there is more kicking room. Other parents say there is too much pull on the shoulders with a backward facing child; she is not close enough to her parent. Some children won't ride backwards unless some other member of the family follows behind to to keep them company. They get lonesome staring at the empty trail.

Whether the child rides forwards or backwards, in the least or most expensive of carriers, she should always be secured in place with a safety strap. If the pack of your choice does not have one, add one before you go out for the first time. Check the strap at intervals on the trail. Straps can work loose, especially with an active child or when the carrier is serving a second generation.

Whatever child carrier you choose, and whichever available options you add to it, there are a few basic qualities to look for in any model. It should fit. Which parent is going to wear the carrier? If you are both going to carry your child and one of you is lots taller or wider than the other, find a carrier with an adjustable harness. Padded shoulder straps and a padded hip belt are absolute necessities. Shifting the weight from the shoulders to the hips makes it much easier to carry heavy loads. Parents who pack their children emphasize that there is a terrific pull on the shoulders; even small babies move around a lot. Padded shoulder straps are more comfortable than unpadded, but they won't help distribute the weight. The hip belt helps to keep the baby's weight firmly centered on your back and also makes it easier to carry more weight under the baby carrier. To add a hip belt, remove the old waist belt, if there is one, and drill a hole through each of the upright supports at the sides of the carrier; attach the hip belt through the holes with the same kind of clevis pins that would hold it to a backpack. A chest strap will keep the carrier from sliding off narrow shoulders and from cutting into your underarms; if your pack doesn't have one, wrap a narrow strap or even a shoelace around your padded straps. Finally, you should be able to get the pack on easily, without any help.

CONSTRUCTING A CARRIER

The two most common complaints about commercially available child carriers are that they do not have enough storage for gear and they are not suitable for the toddler or the larger child who needs to be carried only part of the time. Many parents who cannot find or cannot afford the kind of baby carrier that they want end up adapting an existing model or constructing their own. Starting with a used pack to serve as the base of their new model, parents can get exactly what they want at little cost.

The easiest way to add storage to a baby carrier is attach a bag to the outside. For years, I used a mesh string shopping bag, the kind that housewives in Europe use to take to market, pinned to the back of our carrier. I lined it with a plastic garbage bag to make it waterproof. More permanent storage can be had by sewing pockets to the outer sides of the carrier. You have three sides, you can attach three pockets. The trick is to get the bag off the frame; then you just treat the side like a flat base and stitch a square or rectangle of packcloth to it. Don't stitch the cloth down flat; allow a little fold of material at each side to create a bellows pocket. Unless you're a proficient stitcher, close the pockets with adhesive-backed VELCRO® fastening tape. If you're able to, attach a zipper and even a rainflap.

If you're hesitant about trying this yourself, find a shoe-repair or pack-repair shop that will do it for you. In Seattle, Rainy Pass Repair does custom modifications on packs; they told me that 80% of their business is mailed to them. If you can get the bag off the frame it will be easier to ship to them. You can call them to discuss your needs (see Appendix B).

If the toddler still fits in her carrier bag but the carrier itself rides too uncomfortably for Mom and Dad, then one simple solution is to put the bag on a different frame, one that will transfer more weight to the hips. How you do this depends on the design of your carrier and your new frame. Will the old shoulder straps and hip belt go on to the new frame, or will these be replaced? How was the bag fastened to the old frame? That might determine how you will fasten the bag to the new frame. You can consider using lashing, metal screws, or clevis pins. The family that suggested this also added a big pocket to the carrier bag. With the new arrangement, they not only carry their son more comfortably, but also some of his equipment in the pocket and some of their own lashed on to the larger frame below the carrier.

A small-sized pack bag on an external frame can be converted to a child carrier by cutting two holes toward the bottom for the child's legs. The child rides facing backwards, with extra clothing, diapers, or other soft baggage arranged under and around him to make him comfortable. The bag should be small enough that the child can see over the top; a small baby, even one who was propped up with lots of padding, might not be happy in this pack. If the bag is attached high on the frame, there should be room enough underneath to lash sleeping bags and/or a tent to the frame. These items will also provide a more solid seat for the child.

One family used a pack with double compartments to create a baby carrier for their daughter. On their pack, the upper compartment opens just from the top, so they cut two leg holes in the back and added a flap and a zipper to close them off on trips when the child doesn't go along. The metal frame that holds the bag open makes a convenient anchor for a safety belt to hold the child in place. The little girl rides facing backward in the top compartment, high up where she can see, while the bottom section remains free for storage.

Another family adapted a pack with double compartments whose upper compartment could be loaded from either the top or the back; the back opened with a long, semicircular zipper. They devised a sling seat for the inside of the compartment using a contoured diaper as a pattern, and their son sits with his legs sticking out of the open back. They pinned their seat to the front and back of the compartment, but you could also attach it with big snaps or with VELCRO® fastening. These parents also fastened a safety strap to the bars that held the upper compartment open.

A large pack with a single compartment that opens from the top and the back can be adapted in the same way if the zipper on the back is a two-way. First the pack would have to be loaded carefully about two-thirds full; then the flap should be zipped up on the sides just far enough to cover the cargo. The top of the flap gets pushed through the opening to form a seat for the child. The pack should be loaded so that the child has something soft to sit on, and, if your child is in the early stages of toilet training, put a protective barrier placed beneath him, like a folded diaper and a sheet of plastic. Add a safety strap, of course. (The parents who suggested this method assured me that it worked for them. If you have concerns about the zippers staying in place, you might want to pin the pulls at the right level, or pin across the zipper to keep it from sliding open further.)

Baby carrier created in double-compartment frame pack

James Evans

Building a child carrier from scratch is not easy, but that was the solution for one father who wanted to carry an older, heavier child who walked by herself some of the time. The bag he designed was deeper and the frame taller than those found on conventional carriers, so that the child would be held very high and close to the parent, and the thrust of the child's weight would be vertical, down to the parent's hips, rather than pulling back on his shoulders. This carrier had room underneath for lashing two sleeping bags to the frame.

The man who built this carrier emphasized that he did it a number of years ago, when the choice among child carriers was very limited. Baby packs today have better suspension systems and more storage than they used to. Before you undertake to construct your own pack, you should look at what is available in stores, keeping in mind these four guidelines for a good baby carrier: (1) it should hold the baby close to the parent; (2) it should have storage compartments; (3) it should have a place to tie on a sleeping bag; and (4) it should have a padded hip belt and padded shoulder straps.

CARRYING GEAR

Remember the good old days, when you carried everything that you needed for a week or ten days in one neat, compact thirty-five pound pack? Now your wriggly toddler weighs close to thirty-five pounds by herself, and you have to carry her, her extensive gear, and your own as well. Even if you can handle all the weight, the mass of the extra supplies takes extra planning. Where are you going to put it all? Here are some of the tricks parents who hike with small children have learned.

Use every available corner of the baby carrier; clean clothes and diapers can be stuffed under the seat and around the baby. There should be some space left under the baby carrier when it's on you; one or even two fanny packs can be worn under the bag. Or a soft daypack or rucksack can fit in that space. A sleeping bag or a tent could hang there, attached to the frame of the baby carrier by adjustable straps.

If your family is between infants and your sturdy child carrier is temporarily not needed to carry a child, you can use it as a regular backpack. You can pile bags of gear into the empty

**Two fanny packs
below carrier**

Don Silverman

child-compartment; Tough Traveler® makes special bags called, appropriately, "conversion sacks," to "extend hiking use of what-might-have-been-outgrown beloved family hiking products."

A fisherman's vest is a great garment to wear while carrying a baby in a backpack. Most of the vest is made of nylon mesh, so it is cool, and it has lots of pockets in front that can be stuffed with lunch and other necessities.

A parent who is carrying a baby in a sling or a soft carrier in front can still carry a rucksack or a pack on his back. Put the baby on first and then arrange the backpack over the sling straps. You may need help to get it on.

A couple in Seattle developed a method to fasten their soft carrier to the crossbar of an external frame pack. They sewed strong snap hooks to the ends of the shoulder straps and sewed rings midway on the top of the straps. Then they looped the shoulder straps around the crossbar and hooked them to the rings. They tied the side straps of the carrier to the sides of the frame. If you try this, you may not even have to change the fasteners on the ends of the straps of your carrier, depending on what's already there!

Parents have commented that carrying a baby on the chest and a pack on the back is hot, sweaty work. Just carrying a baby around on a normally warm day creates a sweaty bond between parent and child, but when the child is in a cloth sling and the parent has a heavy backpack, the connection is intense and the sling will soon be saturated. A rubberized pad, the kind with a soft fleecy surface on both sides, between the two bodies will protect the sling; these pads can be found in most infants' clothing departments. The pad can be pinned to your shirt or simply laid between sling and shirt.

When the child moves from a front carrier to the back, her baggage can move from back to front. Parents have come up with ingenious ways of carrying a pack in *front* when the baby is riding in back. A rucksack can be worn backwards if the straps are unbuckled, passed through the frame of the child carrier, and

Lois Hancock

Parent who doesn't carry child gets extra goodies

then rebuckled to the sack. The waistband will then be fastened in the back, instead of in the front. The soft carrier, when it no longer holds the baby, can hold her equipment instead. Line the carrier bag with a sturdy plastic bag to keep gear from dropping through the leg holes.

Finally, the partner of any parent who is backpacking with a child will end up carrying a more-than-ordinary load, not just in weight but also in shape, as diaper bags, garbage bags, sleeping bags, and stuff bags full of stuff are lashed to the top, bottom and sides of that once-neat pack.

CHILDREN'S PACKS

When the child gets out of the baby carrier to walk, she will probably want to have a pack of her own. Many children carry or wear a pack to nursery school or day care every day, and there are lots of tiny packs on the market. The pack your child wears on the trail should be made of a sturdy, hard-finished material that will take a lot of abuse and can be cleaned easily. The fancy, fake fur animal or doll packs will last longer if they are saved for the carpool.

How much can children carry? Four-year-old Troy shoulders all his own gear on dayhikes: sweater, jacket, socks, gloves, hat, rainwear, damp-proof sitting pad, sun glasses, flashlight, and a snack. On overnighters, he carries some of the family food as well. Four-year-old Sarah is allowed to take anything she wants in addition to her own small sleeping bag and pad; she usually chooses books and toys. The amount your child can transport may depend not so much on her strength and endurance as on the comfort of the pack that she must carry.

Choose a pack for your youngster that has wide, heavy, padded straps. Some packs for children are sewed with lightweight, narrow straps, more like tapes than straps. These tapes tend to curl up when the pack is worn, and then they cut into the child's shoulders. Uncomfortable rucksacks often end up inside or on top of a parent's pack. You can make shoulder pads that slip onto the pack straps from ¼-inch thick closed-cell foam insulation covered with sturdy cloth. As the child graduates to new packs, the pads can move with her.

Some of the smaller packs that adults use for dayhiking

can be modified to fit older children. If the shortest adjustment of the shoulder straps is still too long for the child, look at the pack to see what can be done to it. If the straps fasten to the bag with grommets and pins of some kind, then add extra grommets. Long straps can be replaced with shorter ones, or you can shorten the long straps with a big tuck, sewn in for permanent adjustment, or pinned in for temporary. Just be sure that the tuck is placed where it won't annoy the wearer. Extra lengths of strap can be used for hip belts. An additional strap across the child's chest connecting the shoulder straps will keep them from sliding off the child's narrow shoulders. (Sometimes little girls wear a shoestring across the back of their swimsuits for a similar purpose.)

A simple pack for a child or for anyone can be made from an old pair of pants. Fill the pants with gear and drape them around the neck, with one leg over each shoulder; the body of the pants, the part that covered the pelvis, will hang on the back. Arrange the contents so that the weight in the pant legs balances the weight on the back and so that nothing in the pack digs in. As the pack hangs in place, the contents will settle. Of course the waist and the feet will have to be closed so that nothing falls out! If you wish to make a permanent pack of your pants, you can put VELCRO® fastener at the waist, or rip out the inseams and line them with VELCRO® fastener. You can keep the pant legs from

Child's pack made from old pair of pants

Don Silverman

sliding off by fastening a couple of ribbons or shoe strings to the legs and tying them across the chest. A pair of toddler's pants with snap-fastened inseams would make a fine pack for a small child if the waist and ankles were sewn closed.

Older children who can carry loads of 10 or 12 pounds are ready for a frame pack. Some companies manufacture child-size packframes, but they are relatively expensive. Adjustable frames are also expensive, but they will fit over a longer period of the child's growth. A poorly fitting frame can be extremely uncomfortable; it would probably be better to give the child a lighter load in a rucksack than a heavier load with a badly fitted frame. If most of your trips are short ones, but you need a bag with a good frame for a once-a-summer long jaunt, consider renting a pack for that trip. Consult your Yellow Pages for rental sources.

My husband, who likes to make and modify our equipment, made packframes out of electrical conduit (lightweight tubing) for our six and eight-year-olds. He copied the design of his own larger frame, but bent the lower part over the hips to fit the children. He put his frames together by welding them, though he could have used metal screws. The kids already owned nylon rucksacks with padded shoulder straps; using those straps, their dad added grommets at the top of the straps and put clevis pins through the grommets to fasten the bag to the top of the frame. New small hip belts completed the conversion. My husband commented years later that it had been a lot of trouble to make the packframes, and he would not recommend that anyone else try it. The kids soon outgrew them, but I found them very comfortable and used them often on dayhikes, until the bags wore out!

A GOOD NIGHT'S SLEEP — TENTS AND SLEEPING BAGS

The family that backpacks together should be prepared to sleep together...usually in close quarters.

TENTS AND SHELTERS

Some backpacking families never set up their tents unless they think it will rain during the night. Lois says that her children like it better when they sleep out. They spread a rain poncho on the ground and lay their sleeping bags on that. The whole family lies close together, and as they drift off to sleep they talk about the stars, and where the bears are sleeping.

Other parents consider a tent to be an absolute necessity on an overnight trip. A baby fighting sleep can crawl around inside a zipped up tent until he falls asleep. Parents outside can keep track of the little darling by watching the bulges of hands and head against the the tent sides. Children who resist going to sleep in strange surroundings often drop off more quickly in an enclosed shelter of some sort.

Don Silverman

Shoes stay out to keep tent clean

A two-person backpacking tent is frequently big enough for two adults with one child. It also will accommodate a parent and two children, the other parent taking shelter under a tarp nearby. However, Roger told me he always takes a tent that is "one person larger" than the number in his group—a four-person tent for three, a three-person tent for two.

A four-person tent is a considerable investment, but well worth its cost to a family that backpacks frequently. Often a good used tent can be found through advertising in a local backpackers' newsletter. Or look for cut prices on tents when a manufacturer changes its design or its colors. Scot bought a tent at half-price in early autumn after it had spent the summer set up on display in an outdoor equipment store.

Although many people who are buying their first tent are tempted to get the largest they can afford, size isn't the only measure of a satisfactory tent. Many backpackers would put light weight ahead of size; the few occasions when you want to stand up in a tent probably won't justify the extra pounds that such a tall tent would require. A basic tent needs to be just large enough to hold all the people who will sleep inside. Packs can be left outside, covered by waterproof pack covers or by plastic garbage bags.

To give your family full protection, your tent should have a rainfly; you can tie and stake a plastic or coated nylon tarp over your tent if yours didn't come with a fly. Another plastic sheet, spread on the ground under the tent, will protect the tent floor from twigs and little rocks, and make the tent last longer.

A few years ago, all tents had a rectangular floor. Today there are dome-shaped tents with round floors, five-sided tents with a storage area jutting out from one end, and boat-shaped tents with extra space extending from both ends. Variations of these shapes appear every year. The best way to choose the shape that's right for you is to crawl inside a lot of tents, look them over, and consider how your family would make use of the space. If there isn't an outdoor equipment store near you that sets up tents for display or if you're shopping from a catalogue, mark off the measurements of each tent on the floor and use your imagination.

Consider the color of the tent you buy, too. Many people say that visitors to the backcountry should be very careful not to intrude on one another's wilderness experience; therefore, their behavior should be as inconspicuous as possible, including using a tent that will blend into the surroundings. They would like all tents to be brown or green or even, as one catalogue showed, camouflage. That's fine for adults who have a sure sense of direction, but when children are playing at a campsite, even close by their tent, they need to know exactly where "home" is. A brightly colored tent—red, blue, or yellow—will be easy to spot in a green and brown forest. So when the children are small, go out with a very visible tent, and later, when they are older, you can hide it with a dull rainfly.

Between sleeping out and sleeping in a tent, a simple overhead fly is the choice of many families. They tie each corner of a plastic or coated nylon tarp to a bush or a tree, and sleep under that. (If the ropes are long enough, trees can be wide apart.) They lie on a ground cloth of similar material. To make a peaked roof that will allow rain or dew to run off the sides instead of collecting in the center, they either run a rope under the tarp and tie the rope ends higher than the corners, or they carefully adjust ropes in grommets along the edge of their tarp to create the proper roofline. If brush is sparse, they make a lean-to of their tarp by anchoring two corners to the ground with stakes or rocks and tying up the two opposite corners. A walking stick or an ice axe can be used as a tent pole to hold up one corner of a tarp.

John and Lisa sewed their own three-sided shelter that combines the advantages of a tent and sleeping out; they can see some sky on clear nights but they're out of the rain the rest of the time. Their shelter is a nylon tarp that reaches the ground on three sides. On the fourth side, the open side, the tarp is held up about two feet off the ground by three collapsible poles. The tarp overhangs the opening to keep the rain out if the wind isn't blowing directly into the open front. It is possible for the children to sit up in their shelter, but not the adults.

Different families use their tents in different ways. Some parents of one put the child in the middle, between the adults. Others, who choose a long, narrow tent, put the child across the bottom of their tent. The two-person dome-shaped tent is popular with many families who have two small children; they put one child on each shorter side and reserve the long center section for the adults. Other parents say they put their kids on the side because they are less likely to jostle them and wake them up when they themselves go to bed later if the kids are somewhat

Just a tarp, two poles, and some rope

John Stevely

Goldie Silberman

Tying a bell to the tent zipper as an alarm

out of the way. I talked to one mother who always sleeps across the entrance to their four-person tent in case their child wakes up and takes a notion to explore; a three-year-old who wanders through the house at night just might do the same thing on a camping trip, especially if the moon was big and bright. Beth had the same concern; she ties a little bell to the zipper of their tent so she will be awakened by anyone leaving the tent.

Like the child who wanders, the sliding child is probably better contained in a tent at night than allowed to sleep out or under a fly. Outside, the slider moves around as he sleeps, and slides off the ground cloth onto the ground. Robb reported that they bought their first tent when they grew tired of waking several times during the night to pull Daniel back under the tarp. Now they camp in a new tent with a sewn-in floor.

A child who has never spent any time in a tent may be very unhappy if he is expected to go to sleep in this strange, new place, even if his parents are with him. Emily fussed all night long the first time she was taken out. When they came home, her parents set up their dome tent in the family room, and she ran in and out of it for a week, even taking her naps on the floor. Next time they went out on an overnighter, the tent was "home," and she had no problems sleeping there.

It's a good idea to set up your tent indoors or in the backyard before you take it out in the wilds. You may even want to sleep there for one night. It gives the kids a chance to get used to the tent, and it gives the parents a chance to see if their plan for arranging bodies and sleeping bags in the tent really works. One old-timer suggests that a new tent should be set up for rain and then squirted with a garden hose from every direction, to test how it will stand up in a heavy downpour. You may find that a seam or two needs additional water proofing.

THE TENT SITE

Everyone looks for a level place to set up the tent, of course, but old hands at choosing a tent site also have a certain backwoods wisdom that your family can use too. For example, sleeping under the trees gives more protection from weather than an open meadow, but there are more insects under the trees than out in the open. Hikers in an area with lots of mosquitoes will need some sort of protection from them, and a breezy site will help keep them away. Test the direction of the wind when you set up your tent; if the wind is blowing straight at the entrance to your tent, you will be colder at night, and if it starts to rain, you might get wet. Sometimes a patch of low-lying, level ground that looks like a terrific spot turns out to be a dried-up puddle; be sure your tent site is not going to be flooded if it rains. Other backpackers who share your campground may be trying to preserve an illusion of being alone in the wilderness; try to choose a campsite that is not close to another tent, and place your tent out of the direct view of other parties, if possible.

Families who hike where the nights are warm and dry don't have to worry about dew, but the family that plans to camp in the mountains or in cooler climates should be aware of conditions that bring heavy dew, especially if they plan to sleep out without a tent. I asked a weatherman at my local television station to explain in simple language how dew is formed. First he told me about *dew*; dew is water vapor from the air that has condensed in the form of drops on objects that are colder than the dew point. Then he told me about the *dew point*, the temperature at which moisture in the air begins to condense. At night and under an open sky, objects on the ground lose heat fast and become colder than the air around them. When their temperature drops below the dew point, they become covered with dew. Dew is more likely to form on still, clear nights than on windy or cloudy nights, because objects cool down faster on still nights. A cloudless, starry sky is tempting to the family that wants to sleep out, but an unprotected sleeping bag can get soaked if the temperature outside of the bag falls below the dewpoint. However, if the bag is set under trees, the branches will afford enough of a roof to slow down the loss of heat and the bag may stay dry. My weatherman warned that in the mountains, especially, it is highly likely that there will be dew at night; he suggests that everyone who goes out to camp should plan to sleep under some kind of shelter. In the Northwest, where I live, packs and bags left out all night will also be soaked, unless they are covered by some kind of pack cover, like a big garbage bag. Families new to backpacking should ask around before they spend a night in the open to find out what experienced hikers in their area do.

Here are some other considerations for choosing a campsite: there should be a water source near by; and it should be relatively easy to reach the water; there should be no dangerous drop-offs or caves to put your kids at risk; if you are near a lake or a river, you should follow the park or wilderness rules on proper distance from the shore for a camp; and if the park has designated campsites, don't camp in an undesignated area.

SLEEPING BAGS

It's possible for a child to bunk with one of his parents in one sleeping bag, and even easier for the child to sleep with both parents if they have bags that zip together into a double bag. Nursing mothers report that sharing a sleeping bag with the baby is convenient for middle-of-the night feedings. However, there are some disadvantages to sharing a bag. A light sleeper, either a child or one of the parents, may find the close contact with another person disturbing. If the child wets the bed (and sometimes even older children do this in strange surroundings), there is no warm, dry bag for parent and child to move to. Furthermore, many parents are concerned about accidentally rolling over on a baby, and they lose sleep worrying about this.

In very mild weather, a snowsuit or a heavy blanket sleeper could suffice for a warm place for a child to sleep. A small baby can sleep snugly zipped up in a parent's warm parka, with the sleeves folded beneath or turned inside for extra insulation. Some families have found that the parka "sleeping bag" works well for the baby's first year. One young family backpacking with a tiny baby wrapped her up in receiving blankets, an adult-sized flannel shirt, and a wool sweater. They put the little bundle into a sleeping-bag stuff sack, and their daughter slept peacefully all night with her father in his sleeping bag.

Eventually, however, parents will have to plan for some kind of separate sleeping arrangement for each child.

There are commercial sleeping bags made for children. Bags filled with goose down are the lightest, warmest, most expensive, and most fragile; if a down-filled bag gets wet, it is no longer light and warm, but it is still just as expensive. A wet down bag must be handled carefully to avoid damaging the down and the inner construction of the bag. For a child who may occasionally wet his bed, a better choice of bag is one filled with a synthetic substitute for down that is almost as light and as warm, but much less expensive. Synthetics, sold under such brand names as PolarGuard®, Quallofil® and Hollofil®, are machine-washable and can be wrung out and dried out a bit in camp if they get wet. In addition, synthetics are warm even when wet.

There is no standard way for rating the size of children's sleeping bags. In the Campmor catalogue, bags are rated according to the height of the persons who will use them; I found there a hooded child's bag rated to 4'8". The Tough Traveler company makes two bags for kids with "high-tech insulating fill" and "semi-hoods." Their Baby Bear model fits kids up to three years old. Their Growing Bear comes with two extensions to adjust as the child grows from 3' to 4'10"; the company claims it will fit up to ten-year-olds. The L.L. Bean Kids' Catalog shows bags 60" long without hoods. None of these bags is inexpensive, but for the family of frequent hikers with more than one child, the investment might be worth it. (See Appendix B to contact these companies.)

Parents who hesitate to invest in a child-size new bag have come up with many suggestions for creative sleeping arrangements for their offspring. A climber's "elephant foot" bivouac bag makes a fine sleeping bag for a child; this bag, intended to cover an adult to the waist, is just the right length for a child.

A sleeping bag can be the easiest sewing project imaginable; it can be all straight seams. Careful shoppers may be able to find the makings for a sleeping bag in a second-hand or a thrift store. An adequate child's bag can be fashioned out of a used full-sized bag. John and Lisa acquired an old sleeping bag with a zipper extending halfway down one side. They cut about two feet off the bottom, resewed it, and presto—a child's sleeping bag. A double comforter can be folded in half and a long zipper or VEL-CRO® brand hook and loop tape installed along two edges to make a sleeping bag suitable for two small children. Child-sized sleeping bags can also be made of cotton sheet-blankets and wool blankets folded and sewn together.

A novel bag that Judy constructed for her daughter is made of light cotton quilting, a fabric intended for quilted bathrobes, on one side, and wool blanket on the other; on warm nights, the child sleeps on the heavy side with the light covering over her, but on cold nights, the wool side is up and the light side down. A more modern version of this bag could use cotton or nylon quilting lined with Hollofil® or Thinsulate® for cold nights, with medium-weight fleece for warmer nights. If there is no shop that sells yardage for outdoor gear in your area, you can call Seattle Fabrics or the Malden Mills outlets (see Appendix B). You might be surprised by the variety of materials that are available.

Of course, another alternative is to purchase adult-sized bags and let the children grow into them. Many parents do this. Some bags are designed for shorter people, and they would serve a child into the teens, at least. In mild weather a child may be comfortable in a large bag, but on cold nights he may not be able to generate enough body heat to warm all the space in the big bag. In that case, fold back the unneeded bottom of the bag and tuck it under him for extra insulation, or tie up the foot of the bag so there's little air inside.

The sleeping arrangement you finally decide upon for your child will be based on a number of considerations. These include the cost of materials or of finished bag, the time and skill involved in making a bag, and the weight and bulk of the finished product. Whether a parent or the child carries the bag, it should be as light and as compressible as possible within the family budget. That means that one family will buy their child an adult-sized synthetic-filled sleeping bag, while another family goes out with wool blankets hemmed to fit their child. Whatever you provide for your child to sleep in, make sure that he is not allergic to the insulating material. Some parents have found that their children are allergic to down. Other kids react to wool and other natural fibers.

LINERS

Small children often sleep in a "bottoms up" position and have a difficult time staying inside a sleeping bag. Commercial bags with satin-y linings are particularly slippery. It's not unusual to awaken and find a child sprawled on the floor of the tent, completely out of his bag. Over-the-foot sleeping garments, like blanket sleepers, help keep such kids warm. Lining the floor of the tent with foam pads will also provide more insulation from the cold. Adding a flannel liner to the bag can help keep the child inside. It can be removed periodically for washing. Flannel liners can be sewed at home or purchased in outdoor stores. Some parents suggest sewing patches of VELCRO® fastening to the sleeping bag and to the child's sleepers. Or, if your tent is large enough, you can try to fence in your young "floater" by using two packs and a corner of the tent.

A waterproof sheet or pad inside the sleeping bag under a baby or an older child will help prevent damage to the bag in case of diaper overflow or middle-of-the-night accident. Rubber pads with flannel on both sides and quilted pads can be found in the infaxnts' section of most department stores. Plastic sheets, folded receiving blankets, or extra diapers can also be used. The sheet or pad can be pinned, sewed, or just slipped into place. Of course, the urine, which must go someplace, will soak into the child's sleeping clothes; you'll have to be prepared to change them. A sleeping bag with a two-way zipper or a VELCRO® fastening that allows the bag to be opened from the bottom allows diaper changes without taking the baby out of the bag.

PADS AND MATTRESSES

Although some hardy souls head out with just a sleeping bag, most backpackers also carry a mattress, pad, or combination of the two. A sleeping bag works by creating a layer of warm air above the sleeper; the part of the bag under the sleeper gets compressed and doesn't keep the cold out as well. The bag is also of little help for softening the hard ground and the occasional twig underneath the sleeper.

An air mattress will provide adequate cushioning, but it does not insulate the sleeper from the cold; in fact, an air mattress does the opposite. It acts as a heat sink, pulling warmth from the body into the mattress. A thick pad, especially if it is closed-cell foam, will keep the cold in the ground and the warmth in the body, but unless it is a very thick pad—an inch or more—it is not an adequate cushion. Some hikers carry both an insulating pad and an air mattress, laying the pad on top of the mattress to block the cold air mass from their bodies. There are short mattresses and pads made for backpackers that extend just from the knees to the shoulders. There are also more expensive self-inflating thermal pads that combine the insulating function and the cushioning function.

Most parents carry some kind of cushioning and insulating combination for themselves, but just insulation for their children. A popular choice is a piece of closed-cell foam no more than one-half inch thick, cut to the child's size. Ensolite and XPE are two well-known brands of foam. Look in the Yellow Pages of your telephone directory under Foam for a source near you.

Sleeping on the ground doesn't seem to be a hardship for children, as long as they don't get cold. Because they are lighter, children don't press into the ground as much as their parents do. Maybe children who are not given cushioning when they are small will have learned to do without it when they are grown.

In many families, the child's pad for sleeping, rolled and strapped, is the first thing he carries for himself when he gets his own backpack.

THE KITCHEN ON
YOUR BACK —
FOOD AND COOKING

On a flat rock in front of their tent, a woman is preparing Eggs Benedict for her family's breakfast. Out of sight but not far away, in front of another tent, another family is having dry granola and hot chocolate for breakfast.

The differences in the way families choose to backpack are nowhere more apparent than in the foods they prepare and eat in the wilds. Some families like to eat the same foods that they eat at home, to keep mealtime as normal and familiar as possible. Other parents like to make backpacking special and different, so they serve foods that they *never* eat at home. Some families are more concerned about nutrition on the trail than they are at home, because of the extra demands that hiking makes on their bodies. Another family eats lots of junk food on their jaunts, because they like junk food, because they don't ordinarily have it, and because they consider it their reward for the hard work of hiking. One family wants their wilderness experience to be as uncomplicated as possible; they carry a limited number of simple, wholesome foods and eat the same things at every meal. Another family tries to prove that they can overcome the limitations of the wilderness, so they fix Eggs Benedict on a camp stove.

Beginning backpackers, leaving their cars at the trail-head, have mixed feelings of fear and pride as they realize that every meal for the next 24 or 48 hours must come from the packs they're carrying. These packs contain both the larder and the kitchen. Beneath the proud feeling that they will be able to survive on just those supplies that they can carry on their backs, there's always a nagging fear that some vital ingredient or some essential tool was left behind. How can parents use their limited kitchens most effectively?

Families with small children, on their first outings, should not try to prepare elaborate meals in the wilds. Fancy meals come with experience. The best foods to take on hikes with children are those that are quick and simple to prepare. Children who have worked up good outdoor appetites on the trail do not like to wait a long time to eat. Parents tired from their hike do not feel like fussing with complex meals. For your first trips, choose menus based on dry, ready-to-eat foods or dried foods that require only the addition of cold or hot water.

You can find an impressive array of foods to take hiking in an outdoor store, but with a little searching you can find an even greater number of appropriate foods in your supermarket. In one afternoon's stroll up and down the aisles, I found all kinds of lightweight, quick-cooking rice and pasta dishes, instant puddings, complete pancake mixes, sturdy cookies and crackers, tasty spreads—all suitable for carrying in a pack. In the so-called "natural foods" section I found bean dishes that cooked in just 8 minutes, and couscous mixes that were ready even faster. Some of the foods need re-packaging; the soups and ramen noodles in individual styrofoam cups are too bulky for backpackers, but transferred to a zipper-topped plastic bag, they take up hardly any room at all.

That zipper-topped plastic bag is the greatest invention for your kitchen. It comes in several sizes. It scrunches down to just the size of the goods inside—no wasted bulk. It's so sturdy you can blend your pancake or dumpling mixes right in the bag. And you can wash it out with hot, soapy water when you get home and use it again and again!

Talking to lots of parents about the foods that they eat when they backpack, I'm sure I discovered something for everyone. Here are their suggestions:

BREAKFAST

The quickest and easiest breakfast is the same thing in the woods as it is at home: cold cereal. Many parents repack Cheerios® or Chex® (or some other cereal that can be eaten easily as finger food) into a sturdy lightweight container, and serve it with fruit drink or milk and dried fruit—raisins, apple chips, date bits, apricots—first thing in the morning. Cooked cereal with dried fruit and hot cocoa is another popular breakfast. Different kinds of cereals and chocolate milk powder can be purchased in individual portions in most supermarkets. Children enjoy opening and stirring their own packets; some packages are printed with cartoons or animal pictures that can create a diversion while you wait for the water to boil. Some cereals will have their raisins, dates or other fruit already added when you buy them; plain cereals can be enriched with fruit, or you can eat the dried goodies while you wait for the cereal.

Packets that you prepare yourself are less expensive than those you buy, and they offer more variety. Measure the amount of dry cereal you need for one serving into a small plastic bag with a zipper closure; add a small amount of sugar, some cinnamon or other seasoning you like, a handful of raisins or other

Bananas—
simple and
healthful

Goldie Silverman

fruit of your choice, and some instant dry milk. Zip the bag closed. At breakfast time, empty the package into a cup, add hot water, stir, and enjoy.

Or prepare the whole family's breakfast at one time by packing their cereal, fruit, and dry milk all together in one plastic bag. Mixing the dry powder into the cereal is one way you can be sure your child gets enough milk; of course, you can carry instant dry milk or UHT milk for drinking, too (see MILK later). You can create your own breakfast treat by combining instant milk and different kinds of cereals—oat flakes, wheat flakes, barley flakes—and then adding a variety of dried fruits and nuts or seeds. Some families use granola or Grape-Nuts®. Before you leave home, figure out the amount of water that you will need to add to your cereal and milk, write it on a small piece of paper, and pack it in with your cereal. Then in the morning you won't have to guess how much water to add.

Instead of cereal, some families like to have a nourishing cookie with milk or fruit drink for breakfast. You may have your own recipe for a cookie that isn't too sweet, travels well, and contains good whole grains, milk and fruit, but if you don't, here's one family's favorite:

Breakfast Oatmeal Cookies

Combine 3 cups of quick cooking oatmeal with 1½ cups *each*: unsifted white flour, whole wheat flour, and brown sugar. Add 1 to 2 teaspoons grated nutmeg, 1½ teaspoons baking soda, and ¼ cup instant nonfat dry milk.

Cut in 1 cup soft margarine (2 sticks). Do this with a food processor if you have one with a large bowl; otherwise, use a pastry blender.

Make some sour milk by putting 1 or 2 tablespoons of lemon juice or vinegar in a cup measure and filling the cup with milk. Let it sit for 5 minutes to "clabber." Then pour the milk over the cereal and mix well.

Stir in 1 cup dried currants or other chopped dried fruit. At this point you will have a large bowl of crumbly dough.

Drop the cookies by tablespoonfuls onto a lightly greased baking sheet, or if the dough is too crumbly, press each tablespoonful into a ball. Use the bottom of a small glass dipped in milk to flatten the cookies. Bake at 350° for 12 to 15 minutes, until cookies are lightly brown around the edges. Store in an airtight container to keep them soft. These cookies can be frozen.

The Marshalls' favorite breakfast is frozen waffles. They carry the waffles in the waxed cardboard package they came in. Even after a day in a pack, the waffles are still whole. Sometimes this family toasts their waffles on their lightweight camping griddle, and other mornings they heat them on the lid of the pan that boils their water for cocoa and coffee. They make a topping for the waffles by adding warm water to freeze-dried applesauce.

The Evans family cooks freeze-dried rice pudding from the outdoors store for breakfast; you can make your own rice pudding from instant rice, powdered milk, sugar, and raisins. Another family purposely cooks more than they can eat in the evening, and then has the leftovers from dinner in the morning. A third family eats the same food for every meal on the trail: peanut butter or cheese with a good, dense, wholesome bread; and fruit, fresh on their first days out and dried as the week progresses.

If you want to try something a little more elaborate, if your children are able to wait longer, or if you are well-organized enough to start breakfast while they are still sleeping, you might surprise your family with eggs or pancakes for breakfast. Just be sure before you leave home that you have the proper pan to cook them in. For cooking eggs, you'll need a lightweight backpacker's frypan; for the pancakes, the frypan or a lightweight griddle. Pancakes or fried eggs require a spatula.

There are many dried egg preparations available in outdoor stores that turn into fancy omelets, or you can buy a plastic egg holder that cradles fresh eggs in your pack. Bacon is available in cans. If pancakes are your choice, make sure that you buy a complete pancake mix, one that doesn't need anything added to it except water or milk. In the same way that you pack the cereal, measure the amount of pancake mix (and dry milk) that your family will need into a plastic bag, zip it closed, and add a note that tells you how much water to add. If you believe the plastic bag is sturdy enough, you can mix the batter right in the bag. Otherwise you'll need some kind of mixing bowl. Pancakes are nothing without syrup; you can transfer one breakfast's quantity of your favorite to a plastic bottle, sealed in a zip-top plastic bag; you can buy a freeze-dried syrup that you must reconstitute in a second bowl or container; or you can mix brown sugar with warm water and a little cinnamon.

At the upper end of elaborate breakfasts, Eggs Benedict will probably not become a favorite of families with small children, but here's how one intrepid cook did it. First, she prepared Hollandaise sauce from a mix in a small saucepan on her backpacker's stove. She covered the pan with a lid, put a wool hat over the whole pan to keep it warm, and set it aside. Then she toasted some English muffins on her lightweight griddle, wrapped them in foil, put another hat on them, and set them aside. Next she warmed ham slices on the griddle, and then she fried fresh eggs on the same griddle. Then she put them all together: for each serving, she topped an English muffin with a slice of ham, then an egg, and finally a covering of Hollandaise. The classic recipe calls for poached eggs rather than fried, but nevertheless she was proud of her accomplishment—although she says she will probably never repeat it.

LUNCH

There is less temptation to try elaborate preparations at lunchtime, since lunches are usually eaten on the trail. Even very small children should have no trouble eating the kinds of finger foods that are popular at this meal. Supermarkets can supply a wide variety of crackers or dense breads, jerky or dried sausages, hard cheeses or cheese spreads, meat and fish spreads in cans, peanut butter and jelly, even Mexican bean dip. Peanut butter and jam can be combined in one small plastic container; carry only as much as you need. The Jeffersons spread their P.B. and J. on tortillas. Hard-boiled eggs in the shell travel well. Our family favorite lunch is individually wrapped string cheese or mini-Babybel cheeses in bright red, yellow, or brown wax coats. My grandson prefers "devil meat"—Underwood brand meat spreads with a bright red devil on the label.

Most overnighters spread their cheese or peanut butter on Melba toast or a cracker at lunchtime (bring a spreading knife!). Crackers should be carried in their cardboard box or transferred to a rigid plastic box to prevent crumbling; choose thicker crackers, which travel better than delicate, thin ones. The same rule holds true for cookies; thick bars like fig newtons travel better than thin, crisp cookies. One exception to the rule of not carrying sandwiches overnight is the Williams family; they take bagels and cream cheese for lunches, enough for their entire trip. They slice, spread, and wrap their bagels before they leave home, and this lunch stays fresh in their packs for several days. On longer trips, they omit the cream cheese, slice the bagels, and freeze them. They carry hard cheese, and they say their lunches stay fresh as long as ten days.

Fruit is an important part of most families' lunches, either as leathers or as dried or fresh fruits. Many families carry apples and oranges in their packs, in spite of their bulk. Grapes, washed and with the stems removed, travel safely in a wide-mouthed plastic bottle. Cherries and strawberries can be carried the same way. Such small fruits are better with small children, according to Anita, because a child can eat just *one* grape and leave the others for later; it's not as wasteful as taking two bites from an apple that he can't finish.

Some families who say that they really need fresh vegetables also carry carrots, cucumbers, or zucchini. That is not to say they carry a package of carrots or a pound of cucumbers; the family will share a few carrot sticks for lunch, or one cucumber. Baby carrots are particularly handy and popular. Many people who crave something fresh and green sprout their own seeds on the trail. Mung bean and lentil seeds sprout in the dark, so they're carried in a waterproof container in the pack; alfalfa seeds, which need sunlight to develop, are carried in a little mesh bag hanging from the pack. Start the seeds at home a day or two before your trip so they'll be just right when you want them. Then put a few sprouts on top of your cheese or meat spread.

Fruit-flavored drinks are very popular in warm weather. In cooler weather, many families take out their stoves to include hot soup in their lunches. Dried soups can be purchased in individual packets or in family sizes. The larger size necessitates getting a saucepan out and dirtying it, while the single serving can be prepared in a cup. Other hot drinks are nice for lunch on a cold day, too, like cocoa or fruit-drink mix prepared with hot water. Fruit-flavored gelatin dissolved in hot water is another good cold-weather drink, rich in protein. On short dayhikes, some carry a large thermos bottle of hot water.

Many dayhikers carry homemade sandwiches, ready to eat, and fruit juice in individual boxes, but these lunches are fragile and need to be packaged carefully. They take up too much space in a pack to be part of an overnight menu.

DINNER

In those few areas where open fires in fire pits are still allowed, the favorite dinner is the old favorite, roasted hot dogs. For most other families, dinner on the trail could be re-named "one pot time." There are many, many choices of freeze-dried dinners in outdoor stores. It's easy to see why those goopy combinations of sauce, protein, and noodles or rice are so popular. They save work for the cook and the clean-up person both. (I like the kind that can be cooked by adding hot water to the bag the dinner comes in; then clean-up is easiest of all.) Sticky dinners are easy to feed to the baby who still is spoon-fed, especially when he is not constrained by a high chair or feeding table. The toddler who feeds himself has an easier time with combined foods than with hard foods that have to be picked up with a fork.

Supermarkets have easy-to-prepare dinners too. There are many choices available that are much less expensive than the freeze-dried dinners. Macaroni and cheese is a classic. Look for other kinds of instant dinners in foil or cardboard packages on the shelves with rice and pasta, and in the ethnic food section.

Was he carrying her when the fish bit?

Patty Leidig

Retort foods—meals sealed in foil that are heated by boiling in the package—are another possibility from the supermarket. Some campers add a can of tuna or chicken to the basic dish.

If you choose a dinner from a supermarket, be sure to read the instructions carefully so that you bring all the ingredients you need to make it complete. You won't be able to run out to get hamburger or milk when you're cooking in the woods. You should also check the required cooking time; if a dish takes 45 or 50 minutes to be edible, you will have to carry enough fuel to keep your stove running that long. I set a limit of 15 minutes of simmering for my dinners, but I prefer the kind that can just be brought to a boil and then set aside. Whether you buy your dinner at the outdoor store or the supermarket, look to see how large the portions are. Labels can be misleading. Serves 4, when each serving is only 6 ounces, won't do in the wilderness. Look for dinners with the largest per person serving, or carry extra meals. If the dinner comes in a bulky cardboard box, re-pack it in a zipper-top plastic bag. Don't forget to include the directions.

For babies and young children, a problem with many prepared dinners—either the kind especially for backpackers or ones from the supermarket—is the excessive amounts of salt and spices in them. If a child is not used to a lot of seasoning, introducing it in the woods is not a good idea. The child may not like it, or he may not be able to digest it. When the family dinner is going to be spicy, some parents carry a different dinner for the youngest child, something in a jar from the baby food section of the supermarket. Gerber Baby Products makes ready-to-eat combinations of rice or noodles with meat for older children called Gerber Graduates®; other manufacturers may have similar products.

Some families reject the prepared dinners outright. Many families are cutting down on salt. Packaged backpackers' dinners tend to be expensive. Some people like to eat the same foods when they are camping that they eat at home. For any of these good reasons, many parents develop their own dinner recipes based on easily available, lightweight ingredients.

Health-food and ethnic stores are good sources of foods to take backpacking. A basic dinner should consist of a starch, a protein, and a sauce. Starches that cook quickly include small noodles, ramen, dehydrated potatoes, instant rice, bulgar wheat, and couscous. Such complex carbohydrates are the wide base of the food pyramid, the fuel that keeps us moving, so eating lots of starches while we're hiking is good for us! Canned or dehydrated meats or soybean meat substitutes can be added to a starchy base and seasoned with a favorite sauce mix. A packet or two of dehydrated soup in the one-cup size is another way to season; use dried tomato soup for a quick Spanish rice or a bean dish, or any of the chicken soups to flavor a chicken-noodle casserole. Again, read the labels carefully; if your meat or meat substitute must be soaked in warm water for 15 minutes before cooking, you may want to plan something else to eat—perhaps a cup of soup—while you're waiting. Look for sauce mixes in salt-free or low-salt versions. If the sauce is too powerful, use less than a full package. Some parents set aside their child's portion of dinner before they add the spices to it. Robb said his toddler doesn't like hot food—neither spicy-hot nor temperature-hot. So her unseasoned portion is set aside to cool while her parents' dinner gets seasoned and hotter. If you have a fussy eater who doesn't like her food all mixed up, set aside a portion of plain rice before you add the meat and sauce.

Dried vegetables are another commonly found ingredient that you can use in camp. "Soup Greens" is the name of the Schilling® brand of combined dried flakes of onions, green peppers, carrots, tomatoes, and celery; it can be found in the spice section of the supermarket. The same section should hold jars of dried parsley, onion, tomato, garlic, and green pepper, if you want to make up your own blend. Don't carry the bottles in your pack! Re-pack the flakes in a plastic bag or mix them right in with your rice or grains. For seasoning or color when you cook, carry tomato paste in a tube.

You can have even greater variety when you dry your own vegetables. If you don't have a food dryer, it's still possible to dry foods in the oven. Lay the washed, sliced vegetables on a rack and leave them in an oven set at 100° overnight or until they are done. Leave the door of the oven open a crack so air can circulate. The finished foods should be crisp and chewy, and they will be much smaller than they were when you started. Dried apple, zucchini, and banana slices are our family favorites (see SNACKS, below).

Proteins are higher up on the food pyramid, but still hikers do not want to ignore them completely. When you plan your menus, keep in mind the "complementarity of proteins;" *Diet For*

A Small Planet by Francis Moore Lappe is a good source of information. She explains that some foods that are not complete proteins by themselves become complete when they are eaten together. Then you don't have to add meat or a meat substitute. Beans and rice, potatoes and dairy products, grains and dairy products, all are pairs that complement each other. So if you serve potatoes and cheese, or potatoes mixed with instant dry milk powder, you have your protein.

Dried lentils and dried beans are other good foods to take backpacking. There is no danger of spoilage, and they are light and easy to carry. Ordinarily beans take hours to cook, but if you grind the beans at home in a food processor or blender, they cook much faster. Cooking time for rice can also be cut if the rice is ground at home; that means you can carry brown rice or regular rice, instead of the instant kind.

Many parents carry fresh vegetables in their packs as an ingredient for their special dinners. Some chop carrots, onions, zucchini, and parsley at home and pack them with a little water in a leak-proof container, ready to be added to a casserole or stew. Others carry whole potatoes, carrots, even broccoli, to chop in camp and add to dinners.

Instant dry milk, already mentioned many times in this chapter, is another nutritious ingredient that travels well and can be added unobtrusively to many kinds of dinners. Either sprinkle a little milk into the pot each time you cook, or add the powder to the other ingredients when you put your dinner together at home. If your child doesn't like the taste of reconstituted dry milk, she can get her milk in her soup or her cereal. (I carry low-fat dry milk, rather than nonfat; the little bit of fat makes it a little more palatable.)

The dinners listed below are only a few of the many combinations that backpacking families have developed. Instructions are brief. It's up to you to figure out the right amount of water to add to each dinner, based on the ingredients you are using and the number of servings you are planning; do this before you leave home.

Recipes for Dinners

1. Cook chopped fresh vegetables in a little oil until they are tender. Add two packages of ramen noodles, but only one pack of seasoning. Add boiling water, and just before serving stir

in a can of tuna or chicken, drained and cut up.

2. At home, combine biscuit mix with instant dry milk in a zipper-topped plastic bag . In camp prepare dried-vegetable or other soup or freeze-dried stew in a pan. Add water to the biscuit mix right in bag, stir well, drop spoonfuls on the bubbling soup, cover, and steam for 15 minutes or until the dumplings are done.

3. Start with a package of dried cream of chicken soup. Add water. When it comes to a boil, add a cup of small shell noodles. After five minutes, stir in a can of chicken and serve.

4. Combine instant mashed potatoes with instant dry milk at home, and pack it in a zipper-topped plastic bag. In camp, bring some water to boil, stir in the potato-milk mixture, and set it aside under a hat to stay warm. Then cook a pot of mixed vegetables, and just before serving, stir in some precooked bacon bits, real or imitation. Serve the vegetables on top of the potatoes.

5. Prepare instant rice; add a can of minced clams and an envelope of cream of mushroom soup, or combine instant rice with canned chicken and cream of chicken soup.

6. Make a sauce from a package of reconstituted stroganoff mix, Swiss or cheddar cheese, instant onion bits, and dry milk. Serve it over cooked wide noodles or cooked bulgar wheat.

7. Finally, there's the backpacker's Thanksgiving Dinner: mix a package of Stove Top® brand dressing, a can of turkey or chicken, a packet of cream of chicken soup, and vegetables of your choice.

All of these dinners are purposely not highly seasoned; if you wish to add more zing, carry pepper, curry powder, chili or your favorite spicy blend.

Whether you make your own dinners or buy the freeze-dried kind, it's a wise idea to try out a dinner at home before you take it to the woods, to get the proportions right and to be sure that your family tolerates it. Our family made a project of testing outdoor foods to see which ones we would like to take hiking. On one night each week we cooked and ate a different dinner in our backyard. We tried several brands

Cooked to perfection

Wendy Marcus

of beef stroganoff, several kinds of chili, and assorted other main dishes. At the end of that summer we had developed sets of complete menus for a one-night and a three-night trip based on the foods we liked best. After that we never ate those particular foods unless we were on a hiking trip; one of the reasons our kids liked to hike was to eat those special foods.

Of course there is more to satisfying dinners than a goopy main dish. Don't forget desserts. There are puddings that can be cooked and eaten warm, and instant puddings that can be prepared by shaking them in a sealed plastic container. If you remove the puddings from their boxes at home and re-package them with the right amount of dry milk, then all you have to add in camp is water. Gelatin desserts will set up if they are placed in a sealed container and set in a cold stream for 2 or 3 hours. Rice pudding, cooked in camp from instant rice, instant dry milk, brown sugar, and raisins, is a complete meal all by itself. Outdoor stores carry lots of fruits desserts, cobblers and crisps, that are quickly prepared. Finally, there is freeze-dried ice cream. (Have you ever left a carton of ice cream in the freezer so long that it turned into a dry, hard lump? That's the first stage of freeze-dried ice cream.) All these are good, high-energy foods that children like.

SNACKS

Snacks should also be chosen for high energy. Most families include a little something to eat as part of their frequent rest stops. Cathy's family calls these "Lifesaver® breaks." David's family calls their snack food "bunny food" because it's just a nibble. Candy, nuts, and dried fruits are all popular snacks. Cheese and meat are good too. Small children like ready-to-eat cereals, like the Chex® varieties and Cheerios®. Some people eat dried vegetables out of hand—peas and zucchini slices are two favorites. These are not packaged, hard, dried peas for soup— they're either freeze-dried or home dried, crunchy peas. Once in camp, popcorn is a favorite snack of many families.

Little sugar hearts, the Valentine kind with the message printed on them, is the favorite snack food for the Marshall family. They buy their year's supply every February, after the holiday when the candies are on sale. They use the hearts as a snack

John Stevely

"O.K. Give me all the snacks."

and as an incentive to move their son along the trail. They promise him a heart at the end of a switchback, or let him choose the color of heart he will carry in each hand. The hearts are not wholesome foods, Ginny admits, but they are quick energy; the only time the family eat junk food is when they are hiking.

For many children, helping to prepare the snacks is an exciting part of getting ready to go backpacking. Children can easily make "gorp" or trail mix or whatever name your family gives to snack mixes. Just put all the ingredients—cereal, dried fruits, candy, or nuts—in a big bowl and let your child mix them up with clean hands. Then scoop the mix into little plastic bags and zip closed. Each child in the family can have her own bag of mix, but hold back some of the snacks for "emergencies," like a rain shower or a hike that's taking too long.

Children can also help with dried fruit and vegetable slices and with fruit leathers. After a parent has cut bananas or apples or zucchini into even slices, the child can lay them on a rack (see drying instructions page 85), ready for the dryer. Fruit leathers are prepared by spreading pureed fruits on a sheet of plastic wrap on a cookie sheet; the leather dries in a slow oven or at room temperature. Children can lay out the plastic wrap and help spread the fruit puree.

When you plan the snacks for your family, use your good sense. Hard candies and nuts are common causes of choking in young children. If your children aren't used to eating these foods, they should not be introduced on the trail.

See that your children drink lots of liquid, too, to prevent dehydration. Plain water is a good drink, but with some children, more water will go down when it's disguised as a fruit-flavored drink. Sugar is an energy food that will help keep the child going, but the sugar also slows down the absorption of water. If you dilute the drink more than the package directs, you can avoid excessive sugar. Some drink additives contain low-calorie sweeteners, but unless you are very worried about cavities, choose the drinks with sugar in them. No one knows for sure that the sugar substitutes are not harmful, and your children can burn up the extra calories on the trail.

Some children don't like lukewarm water or fruit drink. If you're on a dayhike, you can have cold drinks on the trail if you mix up your drink the night before and freeze it; by the time you take your first break, some of it will have melted but it will still be cold, and it will continue to melt at the day progresses. Leave plenty of room in the canteen for expansion before you freeze it; otherwise the canteen will split.

If you're on a hike of several days' duration, try to take your rest stops next to a rushing stream; place your tightly sealed canteen in the water for a short time, and your drink will be much cooler.

"Boy! That tastes good."

Jeffrey Hancock

UTENSILS

Eating these simple meals out in the woods should be as easy as preparing them. You don't need a full set of dishes and silverware. Our family carries a cup and a spoon for each person. We eat everything with these; between soup and dinner, and dinner and dessert, we rinse our cups. We all share fruit drink from the same plastic container it was mixed in. Other families who eat their meals in sequence don't bother rinsing; in the morning they must decide whether to eat oatmeal that tastes of chocolate, or to drink cocoa that has traces of oatmeal in it.

Families who cherish a little luxury and don't mind the extra weight bring a plate or a bowl, a cup, a spoon, and a fork for each person. The plate or bowl should be of light-weight metal or plastic, and it should have high sides to prevent spilling on uneven ground or lap surfaces. If the sides are high enough, the plate becomes a bowl, which a child can handle more easily. The cup should be narrow and deep and have a handle.

The next statement in this book will be construed as heresy by many people, but it is true nevertheless: the Sierra Club type of cup—a wide, shallow, metal cup with sloping sides and a metal handle—is not a good choice for children. This cup tends to spill if it is set down on the least uneven surface, or on a twig or pebble. Furthermore, the liquid sloshes over the sides on the trip between the ground and the lips. When the liquid is hot, the metal gets too hot to drink from. If, finally, the child gets the cup up to her lips, the liquid runs down on each side of her small face when she tips the wide bowl up. Sierra Club cups make good dishes for children to eat from with a spoon. Serve her oatmeal in one, but give your child a deep plastic cup to drink from.

Collapsible cups that "grow" from a little pillbox to a tumbler are lots of fun for children, but not very practical. They collapse or break or both. You can take one along as a toy, but don't depend on it as a utensil.

Before you go out to buy a water bottle for your child, look around your kitchen to see if you don't already have a usable container. Plastic bottles with pull-up tops (for example, those that contained syrup, vinegar, or mineral water) make good canteens for children.

Cooking utensils should be just as simple as eating utensils. Try to get by with as little as possible. If meals cook in the bag or reconstitute in the cup, then all you need to carry is one pot for boiling water. For starters, a clean three-pound coffee can makes a fine pot. A piece of foil will be an adequate lid, and a folded bandanna makes a hot-pot holder.

Selecting a camp cooking outfit is really beyond the scope of a book on backpacking with children, but here's a hint that families can use: to make measuring easier, scratch or etch a line on the inside of a pot or a cup to indicate the half-cup mark, the one-cup mark, and so on. Then you won't have to carry a measuring cup, or concern yourself with errors of measurement.

STOVES

I remember a damp morning when I was trying to boil water over a balky wood fire while three small, hungry children waited for their oatmeal. That was the weekend before we bought our first lightweight stove. There are a few places left in this country where you can cook over a campfire, but even where fires are allowed, many conscientious campers choose not to destroy a part of the scenery—downed wood—by burning it! All travelers into the backcountry should carry a backpacker's stove. What I should have known, waiting for the water to boil so many years ago, was to feed my children foods that don't require hot water.

Like so many other pieces of backpacking equipment, the stove you choose will be determined by considering price, weight, ease of use, and convenience of fuel. Our family chose a stove that burns propane from a disposable cylinder; it was inexpensive and we find it easy to use, but it's not as fast as some other stoves. We rejected the others because we found them harder to use; they had to be primed with an eye dropper and re-fueled by pouring white gas from a separate container. Now there are stoves which don't require priming, or don't need separate fuel containers, or burn kerosene, a fast, cheap, non-explosive fuel—but with each improvement the price of stoves goes up.

A family new to backpacking, not sure that they're going to like it, may not wish to invest in a stove at all. In that case, they can make a tin-can stove which burns twigs and tiny bits of wood—not whole trees. Go to your public library to find the instructions for a tin-can stove; they will be found in Boy Scout

Lath and Sterno stove   **Coffee-can stove**

or Girl Scout manuals, or the Camp Fire Outdoor Book. There are variations in design, but basically a small fire is kept burning in a large can, while water boils in a pan or a second can on top of the "stove." Somehow damp wood burns more readily when it is enclosed in a tin can, but if you want to be sure to have dry wood for your breakfast preparations, gather the wood the night before and cover it with a piece of plastic or put it in a plastic bag overnight. Jellied alcohol (Sterno® is one brand) can also be used in tin-can stoves; you let the alcohol burn right in its can.

Another simple stove can be made of three small squares of extruded metal or plastering lath. When the three pieces are fastened together with wire to make a triangle, they become a rigid support for a cooking pot. A can of Sterno® in the middle of the triangle provides the fuel for this stove. When you have finished cooking, drop the lid back on the can to snuff out the flame.

After a few trips with a homemade stove, when you are sure that you want to be a backpacker, you can invest in a fancier stove.

MILK AND BOTTLES AND BABY FOOD

Everything that has been said here so far has assumed that the children on the trip will eat the same foods that their parents eat. What about the very young baby who hasn't yet graduated to "table" food?

The nursing infant is probably the person easiest to feed on a hiking trip, provided his mother is careful to maintain an adequate fluid intake so she can keep up her milk supply. On a longer trip, she should also take supplementary calcium. Tums® brand tablets are one way of taking calcium on a hiking trip; four to six tablets a day, or two at each meal, is a reasonable amount. (Other brands of antacids won't work because they don't contain calcium.)

The baby who takes milk from a bottle is harder to feed, and his parents have to decide among many options how they will handle his milk. The problems with bottle feeding are the weight of the products, the difficulty of handling them, and the need to keep the milk free of bacteria.

Whether you're out for just a day or for several days, powdered milk or formula can be mixed up in a bottle just before each feeding. On a day trip, bottles can be filled with boiled water at home and sealed tightly; then you can add milk powder directly to the bottle on the trail. In camp, boiled water can be brought from home, or water can be boiled on a stove. Some families boil water at the end of each day, pour it into plastic bottles, and use it that night and all the next day. Enough clean, dry bottles can be brought from home to suffice for a short trip, but they will take up a large share of the space in a pack. More likely, bottles will be thoroughly scrubbed with soap and hot water in camp. Nipples can be boiled over a camp stove. In cold weather, some parents start the day by filling bottles with very hot water and wrapping them in insulating materials; when it's time to mix up the formula, the water has cooled down to just the right temperature. If you use the kind of nurser that consists of a plastic bag in a hard plastic holder, you can bring just one holder, an inserting gadget if you need one, and enough bags to last the trip. In any case, you will need a measuring spoon and a funnel to transfer the powder to the bottle without spilling.

The bottles you make up in camp will be clean but not sterile. No matter how clean they are, the possibility of contamination exists. Warm milk is an excellent medium for bacterial growth. Therefore, parents should not rely on previously boiled water or boiled nipples to assure themselves that the baby can't get any bacteria from the formula. Be very careful not to mix up the formula until you are ready to feed your child. Don't let milk sit around unrefrigerated, and don't give the baby a bottle that was made up a few hours earlier.

If you're really worried about keeping milk wholesome on a trip, give your baby either bottles that were terminally sterilized at home or ready-to-feed liquid formula.

Terminal sterilization is a process like home canning using a hot-water bath. Filled bottles are loosely capped and cooked in a sterilizer for twenty minutes. After the bottles have cooled in the sterilizer, the caps are tightened. These bottles can now be safely stored without refrigeration; you have actually canned the milk.

The same process was used by the company that put up the ready-to-feed formula. These products come packed in 4-, 6-, and 8-ounce bottles, or in 8-ounce cans. All you do is break the seal on the bottle, pop on a nipple, and it's ready to feed. This kind of packaging is expensive and heavy to carry, but maybe the peace of mind is worth it to you.

UHT (ultra high temperature) milk is milk that has been treated to survive for a long shelf life without refrigeration. This milk comes in little boxes that can be found on the shelves of the supermarket, alongside the powdered milk. If you put it in your backpack, make sure it is not in a place where it will be squashed, or you'll find yourself crying over spilled milk. UHT milk is an expensive way to buy milk and a bulky way to carry it, but children who are used to homogenized milk, who may not accept a return to formula or reconstituted dry milk, might drink this product. If the child insists on *cold* milk, wrap the box in a plastic bag and put it in a stream for a short time.

To summarize the milk-feeding situation, the choices cover this wide range: if you want the method that will put the least bulk and weight in your pack, carry powdered milk and the plastic-bag type of nurser, and boil the water that you use for your camp water supply. Unfortunately this method is the most demanding of your time, and it also takes more fuel for your stove.

If you want the method that is the least work, carry ready-to-feed bottles—which turn out to be, naturally, the heaviest, bulkiest, and most expensive products. The methods in between are compromises. Each family will have to decide for itself which factors are most important.

Does it seem as if carrying milk is just too much trouble and you're thinking of staying home? Don't give up. When you feed your baby his solid foods, mix some dry milk into his cereal or pureed fruit, and see that he gets plenty of fluids like water and juice. Some new parents have a hard time accepting this, but a baby can go for several days without any milk and not suffer any damage at all, so long as she gets fluids and other foods. When you offer juices at meals or at rest stops, be sure to give the baby a variety. There are many kinds that come in 6-ounce cans. Sometimes too much orange juice gives a baby diarrhea and a red, sore bottom. Apple juice, which my generation used to *check* diarrhea, is now suspect as a possible cause of chronic diarrhea (see the *American Journal of Diseases of Children*, May 1985). Cranberry and cherry juices, rich in ascorbic acid, will inhibit the formation of ammonia in the baby's urine and so prevent diaper rash.

SOLID FOODS FOR BABIES

The baby's solid foods in camp should be the same foods she is getting at home. Cereals should be repacked into light-weight plastic containers or zipper-topped plastic bags so you won't have to struggle with bulky, opened boxes. Baby foods in jars must be carried in their original, sealed containers; once the seal has been broken the food is not safe from spoilage. After the jar has been opened in camp, it should not be saved for a second meal for the same reason. If you have been accustomed to giving your infant two half-jars of two different foods, consider feeding her a whole jar of one food at one meal, and a whole jar of the other at the next. When you carry glass jars, handle them carefully. Pack them in a space where they are not likely to clunk against something hard, and keep the empties some place where you or a curious toddler can't be cut by them.

Of course, if you know you will be taking your baby hiking, you can also start getting her used to eating table foods early in her life. Just mash up the food you're eating and share it with her.

While you're packing the baby's meals, don't forget her utensils. She'll need a spoon for sure; an unbreakable bowl for mixing foods; a big, washable bib; and some kind of soft cloth for face washing.

AT THE BOTTOM OF YOUR PACK

When you are hiking by yourself, there are some items that don't fall into any easy category but are indispensable. When you take the kids along, they're even more important. At the bottom of your pack, in a pocket, or in some corner, you should find room for these.

FIRST-AID KIT

The first-aid kit you carry for your children is not much different from the standard kit you carry for yourself. Kids are subject to the same problems as their parents—burns, scratches, diarrhea, etc. Parents must be prepared to cope with these ailments on a child's level. Sometimes that means that different medications must be carried for the adults and for the children, or that a different dosage will be given to a sick child than to a sick parent. If you don't already have preferred treatments and products that your family uses for common complaints, discuss what to do with your doctor before you go on your first overnighter. (Taking a first-aid class and reading a good first-aid manual are other ways of preparing yourself.)

I consulted with Katherine Tempest M.D., a pediatrician

who backpacks with three children, on the kinds of complaints parents should prepare for and the remedies they should carry. Although she urged parents to talk to the doctor who knows their children, she did consent to make some general comments. She said that certainly you might have scratches and blisters, so you will want to pack band-aids, moleskin, and antiseptic. A needle and tweezers are handy for removing splinters. Burns are a common accident; treat them with cold water and a clean bandage. If the skin is raw or blisters rupture, apply an antibacterial ointment such as Neosporin or Bacitracin and a protective bandage.

Sunburn is another common problem. Try to prevent it with covering clothing and sunscreen lotion, but also take along your favorite soothing treatment. Dr. Tempest recommends 0.5% or 1% hydrocortisone cream, available over the counter at your drugstore. The lower concentration is just as effective as the higher.

Dr. Tempest also warned parents to exercise caution in the use of insect repellents on children. She gave me a copy of Medical Letter 1985, Vol. 27, pp. 62-64 to read. It said that the chemicals in topical insect repellents (for example, N,N-diethyl-m-toluamide, popularly known as "deet") can be absorbed through the skin. These chemicals have been used for years in low concentrations, but with excessive or prolonged use they could be severely toxic, particularly in infants and children. Now products are coming out that contain much higher concentrations of the chemicals than before, as much as 100%. Even brief exposure to smaller amounts of the new products has caused serious reactions in children and adults.

If you carry insect repellent, use it sparingly and only when you feel it is really necessary. Once applied, insect repellent does not need to be re-applied repeatedly. Look for a product designed for children. In my neighborhood drugstore, I found Skedaddle!®, which is only 6.2% deet, Off! Skintastic for Kids®, only 4.75% deet, and Bug & Sun Coppertone®, a product that combines 15spf sunscreen with 9% deet. I also found a deet-free product by Consep® called Blocker for Kids´™. You can apply these repellents to clothing, but most products warn you not to apply it *under* clothing.

In the health food section of my supermarket, I found a deet-free insect repellent called Buzz Away™. It comes as a lotion, in a combined sunscreen-insect repellent, or in packets of premoistened towelettes. The product contains five different plant oils which the manufacturer's spokesman assured me were all effective, but the listed effective ingredient was 5% citronella. The manufacturer told me that the combination of five oils is just as effective against insects as the low-percentage deet products. (Call Quantum, listed in Appendix B, to find a source near you.) Citronella is an old-fashioned repellent frequently seen as fragrant candles. I found little bottles of citronella oil in the aroma therapy section of the same health food department. You might find other brands of deet-free insect repellent there as well.

Better yet, improvise protection from insects with clothing and mosquito netting. An older child who is walking or riding in a backpack can wear netting draped from a wide-brimmed hat. An infant in a soft front pack can be protected by a mosquito net pinned to the top of the pack and falling over the baby. A folded mosquito net and a few safety pins take up so little space that it's easy to pack them with the essentials. The same protective clothing will also help prevent sunburn. When you believe you must use repellent, apply it to the child's clothing rather than to his skin.

Expect a few insect bites and be ready to treat them. Dr. Tempest gave me several easy-to-use suggestions for treating the stings of bees, wasps, and other insects. The first is to immediately apply a solution of water and meat tenderizer to the sting. (The tenderizer purportedly breaks down the proteins in the insect venom.) Don't prepare the solution at home; mix it when you need it, in a proportion of about a quarter of a teaspoonful of tenderizer to a teaspoonful of water. Just cover the sting, and the pain should stop within seconds. Be sure to buy unseasoned meat tenderizer; the other kind might attract more bees. Other suggestions are to use a drop of household ammonia for any sting, a paste of baking soda and water for bee stings, or a drop of vinegar for wasp or hornet stings. I also found in the health food section of my supermarket Itch Nix™ and Sting Soother™, both natural products made by Quantum (see Appendix B).

Before you take meat tenderizer, an antiseptic, a sun cream, or any other product on a trip, test it to be sure your child is not allergic to it. Rub a small amount on the back of his hand; if the skin reddens, don't use that product.

I also talked to Dr. William Robertson of the Poison Center in Seattle. Dr. Robertson told me to tell parents to read the labels on all products very closely and follow those directions carefully. Whether it's sun block, insect repellent, or anything else, he said, don't use products in ways they were not intended to be used. Above all, he said, keep the product out of the child's mouth, eyes, and nose, and from his hands too, which might find their way to his mouth.

Aspirin used to be an indispensable product in any first-aid kit. Not anymore. Follow your own doctor's advice about medicines for pain, fever, minor aches, and skin irritations. Your doctor may favor different medications for the children's pain and for your pain.

If you're going to be out for a few days, you should have something for constipation and something for diarrhea. If you have a child in diapers, carry a preparation to prevent or to treat diaper rash. Taking a baby's temperature when you're miles from the doctor won't do much good, but if it makes you feel better take along a rectal thermometer. Include in your kit a handbook of first aid and a list of poisonous plants in your area, and instructions on what to do if someone runs through a patch of poison ivy or eats a poisonous leaf. Any medications your child uses for allergies or other conditions should go along too.

Does it sound as if you could fill your pack with nothing but first-aid items? You will if you buy the large economy size of everything. For backpacking, buy the smallest tube of ointment you can find. Other products should be repacked in small plastic bottles. Avoid aerosol cans; they take up too much space, and it's too easy to squirt your children right in the eye. If you do carry spray containers, spray your hand with the product first and then rub it on the child.

Some people believe that perfumed lotions and soaps attract insects; just to be on the safe side, choose the most neutral products you can find. Plain baby oil works as well as lotions, and corn starch is as good as perfumed talcum powder. Whatever products you use on the trail, be sure to keep them out of the baby's eyes, nose, and mouth, and away from his hands, just as you do at home.

SANITATION SUPPLIES

Keeping your children clean on a hiking trip is impossible, of course, but maintaining some standards of hygiene is not. You want to teach your children good outdoors manners, and teaching by example is an easy way to begin.

You'll need to carry supplies for washing dishes and supplies for washing people. Some people save space by using the same biodegradable liquid detergent for washing their dishes and their faces. Others carry a small plastic bottle of liquid soap and a little bar of soap. If your child has sensitive skin, carry a little bar of baby soap just for him—or have the whole family use baby soap on the trip. Unless you're very squeamish, the whole family can share one wash cloth and one small towel. Some families carry lightweight all-purpose paper cloths, the kind you buy in supermarkets, to use for all their washing and drying. They keep their dish cloth separate from their face cloth by using different colors. You can also find soft, super-absorbent backpackers' towels at many outdoor stores.

You'll need something to do your washing in. Many backpackers use their largest cooking pot as their dishpan, and some use it as a wash basin as well. If you might be rinsing out baby clothes, you may not want to use a pan you'll be cooking in. Bring along some kind of lightweight basin. If you don't want to buy one, the bottom half of a one-gallon plastic jug, the kind that bleach comes in, makes a fine wash basin. If you put it in the bottom of your pack and fill it with other goods, it takes up hardly any space at all. If money is of little concern, you can buy an inflatable bucket or wash basin at an outdoor store.

Plastic jug bottom makes a good wash basin

Don Silverman

Plastic bags are an absolute necessity on a hiking trip. Recycled clean produce bags from the supermarket will hold clothing that needs to be kept separate and foods that you've grouped together into meals. More produce bags can hold unburnable garbage, diapers changed along the trail, used toilet paper, and litter you pick up that others have left (you do want to set a good example for your children). Use double bags if you're worried about leaks, and carry the filled smaller bags in one big garbage bag on the outside of your pack where it'll always be handy. A large plastic bag makes a fine pack cover if you leave your pack out overnight. The best kind of plastic bag, my personal choice as the greatest advance for backpackers since I started hiking, is the kind with the top that zips closed. I re-pack many, many items, from food to premoistened towels to used toilet paper in these bags. When I get home, I recycle the bags by washing them in warm soapy water, turning them inside out and hanging them up to dry. Always take a few more bags than you think you'll need; extra bags usually aren't extra at all.

And don't forget toilet paper. Each older member of the family—those who are trained—should carry his own supply, along with a couple of premoistened towels for cleaning the hands. In one family, each member carries his own "bathroom bag," a small nylon sack that holds a personal supply of toilet paper, towels, and whatever other personal supplies that person will need on the trail. The bag fits in a coat pocket. Somewhere in the pack there should be a family supply for replenishing pocket supplies. In many families one of the adults carries a small garden trowel for burying human wastes.

WATER TREATMENT

Once upon a time, a backpacker could safely drink the water from any source so long as it was clear and running fast. Not any more. Today we should assume that every stream is polluted, especially when we take young children along who may have little immunity to the unseen bugs in water. The organisms to worry about are bacteria and protozoa, which are quite large, microscopically speaking, and viruses, which are quite small. Water-borne viruses are not a great problem within the US, but are a concern to overseas travelers. *Giardia lamblia* and *cryptosporidium*, often mentioned in hiking literature, are both protozoa. There are four common ways of treating water to make it safe to drink: adding chlorine, adding iodine, mechanically filtering and/or purifying the water, and boiling it.

The tablet form of chlorine or iodine is the simplest way of adding these products; some of the common brand names that you can buy from your pharmacist are Halazone (chlorine), Polar Pure, and Potable Aqua (iodine). The manufacturers claim that these products protect against *Giardia* and viruses. Water can also be chlorinated by adding a few drops of household bleach to a container of water and shaking it. Iodine can be added by swishing a container of iodine crystals through the water. When the water to be purified is cloudy or has a lot of material floating in it, the amount of chemical must be increased.

Neither chlorine treatment nor iodine treatment can be recommended for water that is intended for babies, small children, or nursing mothers. Too much of either of these two chemicals could be fatal to humans, and babies are especially susceptible. Iodine may enter the milk of nursing mothers. Furthermore, there is some debate over whether chemical treatment is effective against *Giardia*. The efficacy of chemical treatment can depend on such things as the amount of organic material in the water, the temperature of the water, the exposure of the chemical to air, the age of the chemical, and the time that has elapsed between treating and drinking the water.

On the other hand, filtering, if it is done with a fine enough filter, will remove large organisms like *Giardia* from water, but it won't get rid of viruses. To deactivate viruses you need a special purifier that acts upon them chemically. In a backpackers' store or catalogue you will find a large selection of devices that consist of a pump with hoses and filters and sometimes purifiers as well. An intake hose goes from the water source to the filter; an outlet hose carries water from the filter to your clean container. A pre-filter on the intake hose removes large particles from the water before they clog the microscopic filter. (We fastened a new gasoline filter for an automobile engine to our intake hose to act as a pre-filter).

Most people who use these gadgets report that the job is easier if two people work together, one pumping while the other holds the outlet hose in the container for the filtered water; this latter is a good job for a child. He may also want a turn as pumper. If you buy a filter, look for one that is not too heavy, easy to use, easy to clean, and easy to service when the filter needs replacing. In any case, the filter will add weight, bulk, and expense to your backpacker's outfit.

Boiling water for just a few minutes will destroy *Giardia* and other organisms. At sea level, rapid boiling for two to three minutes is enough; increase the boiling time to five minutes at 6,000 feet. Boiling is quick and easy if it is built into your camp routine; after your dinner or breakfast, put a pot of water on the stove and boil enough to meet your needs until you can do it again.. Some people boil their water just before bedtime; they pour the hot water into drinking bottles and use them as hot-water bottles in their sleeping bags. (Put the bottle in a zip-top plastic bag to prevent possible bag-wetting.) Boiling water will increase the amount of fuel that you must carry, but otherwise it doesn't add cost or weight. The flat taste of boiled water will disappear if you pour it back and forth from one container to another several times, or if you add a powdered fruit-flavored drink.

MISCELLANEOUS HANDY THINGS

Veteran backpackers try to leave things out, to make their packs as light as possible; however, when you hike with children, it's not a time to worry about shaving ounces. Among the things that various parents take along when they hike, you will find some that you will consider indispensable and others that you can easily leave at home.

Novice hikers might want to carry along a basic backpacking handbook. Many such books are available in lightweight editions, and they can be worth their weight in freeze-dried caviar! A handbook will help you deal with unexpected situations; it may help solve some of the problems you didn't know you were going to have.

Another little book that belongs in your pack, if you are going hiking on an ocean beach, is a tide table. Hikers have been stranded and forced to wait hours for the tide to go out because they didn't know how to plan their day.

Books in general can be found in many packs. If your child needs to hear a special story in order to fall asleep and you haven't memorized it yet, take the book along. If you expect your kids to nap in camp in the afternoon, take a book along for yourself. Or take a book to help identify flowers, birds, or mushrooms.

Some backpackers carry a walking stick at all times. Mountaineers carry ice axes. Others use a variety of sturdy broom handles, branches, or other strong, straight poles to help them balance while crossing logs or to help support their weight while going uphill. A pregnant woman or a parent carrying an active toddler will be especially grateful for the extra support. An old cross-country ski pole makes a good stick. Grasp the handle at the top to balance while stepping down off high places. Make a second grip by gluing a piece of rubber or plastic foam at a comfortable place, the spot where you grab the pole when your elbow is bent at a right angle.

A container for water—larger than the water bottles in your pack—is useful for carrying the water that you filtered back to your campsite; our family uses clean Mylar inner bladders from wine or juice boxes. We put the filled bladder into a plastic supermarket bag with handles for easier carrying.

Marilyn carried an umbrella for a hike through the Grand Canyon. She used it to keep the sun off herself and her baby in his backpack carrier. Hikers in rainy country might use an umbrella to stay dry if the trail they are on is wide enough and free from overhanging brush. Charley recommends extending a walking stick with an umbrella and draping the whole thing with mosquito netting to provide support, shade, and insect protection all at once. Robin found a clip-on umbrella in a patio furniture shop; she fastened it to Josh's baby carrier to keep them both cool.

Some parents provide each person in their party with a whistle for emergency use only. It takes a few trips to train children not to blow it just for the noise it makes, but once they understand, they accept the whistle and keep it handy. Many parents don't like to put strings around their children's necks for fear of choking accidents if the string catches on something. They pin the whistle to the child's shirt or to the inside of a pocket instead. A string, if used, should be light enough to break under strain. Test the string you choose. Thin nylon cord won't break easily; try cotton instead.

Other parents tie a bell onto their children's packs or shoes. They

Umbrella in Grand Canyon

Jeffrey Hancock

call it a "bear bell." The jingle is supposes to warn wild animals on the trail ahead that someone is coming; otherwise, a startled animal might attack.

Many parents find it practical at some times to tie up their wandering toddlers. Perhaps a family must stop at a site that is just too dangerous for free exploration. Perhaps there is work to be done setting up camp and the parents can't supervise the child's play. Some families carry a child's harness and leash for times like these. Others carry a rope that they tie around the child's waist. The other end of the leash can be tied to a tent stake stuck in the ground if no tree is handy. Try to find a cleared space for the child to move around in, and of course check on him often to see that he isn't all tangled up.

Lots of parents carry extra rope. Jackie carries a jump rope; on the trail, her kids all hold on to it to stay together, and in camp they jump. Jeff carries a small carabiner, that gadget that climbers use to clip onto ropes. He attaches a rope to it to throw over a tree limb when he's hanging his food at night. Don gets his rope up early so his kids can swing on it.

For changing diapers, for resting during the day, or for a dry place to sit, an extra ground cloth goes along in many packs—in addition to the one that goes under the tent. It provides a sort of porch to your outdoor home. Some parents carry a lightweight tube tent on dayhikes, for changing diapers out of the rain or for napping under shelter. Some families carry a little foam pad for each person to sit on.

Don always carries an extra tarp to set up as a rain fly. He brings one extra pole and lots of extra rope so his fly can be tied off to trees or bushes. Don carries his tarp at the top of his pack, so he can set it up first thing on arriving in camp to provide shade or a dry area for his family.

Dark glasses for everyone belong in the pack when a hiking trail will be crossing snow fields. Anthony rejected child-sized sunglasses but willingly wore his dad's old glacier glasses. Cathy found that sunglasses were more acceptable to her child when she added a little strap to hold them on his head. In the L.L.Bean Kids Catalog, I found glacier glasses for kids, just like mom's and dad's. (See Appendix B.)

Bandanna handkerchiefs have numerous uses in camp and on the trail, from wash cloth and towel to emergency sling. A folded bandanna works as a hot pot holder. An open bandanna can be spread over the face of a sleeping child in a carrier to keep sun and bugs off, and a damp bandanna under a hat or around the neck will keep the head cool. Many backpackers knot their bandanna around the shoulder strap of their pack, where it will be handy for wiping forehead and nose. My favorite bandannas are educational; they show animal tracks or skat. I order them from Pangraphics (see Appendix B).

Toys can be found in some packs. Some parents allow each child to take one small toy; others believe there is enough to interest their children on the trail without toys. Peter and Michael carry toy trucks for major earth-moving projects. Sometimes the toy is one that the whole family can share in, like a jar of bubble-making liquid or a kite. Scot brings a deflated beach ball which they blow up in camp. If a child is very much attached to a blanket or a stuffed animal and can't sleep without it at home, it should certainly be brought along on an overnight trip.

Older children, four to seven, like to have something special to carry. Some of them have their own flashlight, canteen, or compass. A little bag for collecting treasures is also fun to have in a state park or national forest, but children should be taught from a very young age that they should take *nothing* from a wilderness area or a national park.

Finally, a checklist of everything you might want to have in your packs will assure you each time you go out that you haven't forgotten anything. Appendix A gives you a start on a list; you can add or subtract to make it your own.

PART III

WHAT TO DO

The weather is lovely as you leave your car at the trailhead. Your clothes are right, your pack is full, all your planning is complete. You should have a perfect hiking weekend.

You should, yes, except that your family isn't perfect. All the physical work of selecting, assembling, and packing everything you could possibly need for two days is not the end of your task. Once you're under way, the real challenge of the trip begins—caring for the kids on the trail and in camp.

GETTING THERE IS HALF THE FUN

Fifty feet from the car, your little one says, "I wanna drink of water."

This is the moment of truth. It is so easy to say, "But you couldn't possibly be thirsty!" Of course the child isn't thirsty. He wants to drink. He wants to try out the canteen, the special cup, the plans that he helped to make. This is the time when the parents must show how good-humored, flexible, and patient they can be. If they feel they must keep urging their children on, the trip won't be fun for anyone. If, on the other hand, the parents adjust to the pace of their children, stop for interesting experiences like drinking from a water bottle, and keep the children entertained on the trail, the hike will be a success for everyone.

Many parents have noted that when a child complains that he is tired, he really means that he is bored. Frequently, a child will drag along, insisting that he can't go one step farther. Then when the family stops to rest, the child is all over the place, romping around.

When John was four, walking along with no pack on a 2-mile stretch of fairly level trail through woods and across meadows, he told his mother he was all worn out. But when they came to the uphill part of the trail, where the boy had to scramble and hold on with two hands in some places, he forgot all about how tired he was and went up the trail like a little monkey.

Most trails are not challenging enough to keep children interested in hiking at all times, so parents must find other ways of entertaining them. Hiking families have developed many favorite devices for keeping the children going. Some of their methods might work for you too.

ENTERTAINING THE INFANT

The infant in the baby carrier is the easiest kind of child to amuse. The motion of being carried and the closeness to the parent do a lot toward keeping her happy. The company of two parents at the same time is a treat, and their singing or conversation is comforting. In addition there is a big, fascinating world to look at. Little things that parents do can make the baby even happier.

If your baby is accustomed to holding her own bottle of milk or juice, tie a bottle to the frame of his carrier. Some models of carriers provide a bottle holder as an option. Be certain that the bottle is made of plastic; a glass one won't last long on the trail. If your infant uses a pacifier, tie that on too. A rattle, a teething ring, or any other favorite toy can be tied on the same way. Check occasionally to be sure that the ties aren't getting tangled; half-inch ribbons are easier to separate than strings.

Fasten something to look at or to grab at on the hat of the parent who is carrying the baby. A dangling red plastic cup, a toy with a bell inside, a bright spot of color—anything that won't tear or break in her hands—will amuse a baby. Don't feel self-conscious about wearing a hat with something crazy on it—one of the nice things about getting away from it all is that no one can see you!

Some parents hand their child things to look at that they pick up along the trail—a rock, a stick, a leaf. Objects should not be so small that they could be swallowed, and plant materials must not be poisonous. If the child is at that stage where he puts everything into his mouth, it is better to stick with safe toys from home and save the natural materials for another trip.

A teething biscuit is always good for concentrating attention. Parents learn to accept the crumbs in their hair and on their neck if it keeps the baby happy.

HOW TO CARRY A CHILD

The parent who is carrying the child must be extra careful of the way she walks. If she bends over suddenly the child could be catapulted out of the carrier right over the parent's head. Even if the baby has a seat belt or harness in her carrier, she could still experience a frightening jerk.

Parents must also look out for low overhanging branches, and branches that spring back across the child after the parent has pushed them aside. Many couples let the parent carrying the baby walk in front so there is always someone behind the child to check on her welfare.

When two parents go out with a child in a backpack carrier, they often find that their loads are very much unequal. The parent carrying the baby not only has crumbs in his hair but also has the pull of the squirming child to contend with. The other pack does not move around by itself, but it may be a lot heavier. Many couples switch packs occasionally to even out the work. (Sometimes they move tie-ons, to adjust to each adult's capabilities.) It's more interesting for the baby, too.

As the child gets older, he will want to walk by himself

A rest break by the creek

Ella Ryan

part of the time and ride in the carrier part of the time. When there are two small children in the family, perhaps ages two and four, the older child may also want to ride part of the time. Many families switch the child that gets to ride. Usually the older child needs a shorter turn in the carrier; sometimes he's just checking to be sure his parents care about him.

KEEPING THE OLDER CHILD GOING

Some children have no trouble going the distance, but they need a little help with the obstacles, like stepping up over big rocks or maintaining their balance on the uneven surface of a trail. One grandmother recommends a "grandmother stick" to help the children feel more secure. She uses her walking stick, but any long, thin branch picked up off the trail will do. An adult holds each end of the stick, and the children walk between them, holding on to the stick with one hand. Jackie's jump rope works the same way.

In many hiking groups the slowest person goes first and sets the pace for the rest. Some families let the youngest walker act as pacesetter. But when there are several children in the family, that doesn't always work. Our family tried to let our children take turns going first, but it didn't work with the wide age spread of our kids. When the youngest was in front, his older siblings complained that he was too slow. When an older child was first, the youngest was furiously frustrated because he couldn't keep up. It seemed wise to separate the children to stop the bickering, so we divided into two groups. One parent walked with the youngest child, and one parent stayed with the older children. When the youngest needed a little boost or a hand to hold back a branch, the parent was able to help him without comment from the others. The fast group stopped frequently to let the slow walkers catch up. Now that our children are grown, we apply the same system to three generational backpacking trips.

TRAIL RULES

Long before the children are ready to hike up the trail ahead of their parents, they must show that they can follow traditional hiking rules. Teach the children to stay on the trail at all times. Show them how switchbacks can sometimes be misleading; it is too easy sometimes to keep walking straight when the trail actually turns back on itself. Beyond the danger of getting lost, you should also teach your children that short-cutting across a switchback creates a pattern of erosion that can wash away the hill, and that the fragile plant life alongside the trail is damaged by walking on it.

Young children should be taught to stay within sight. Older children must stay within earshot and must call in often. As they grow older the distance they can shout increases, and so does the distance they may go ahead. If a fast group—one parent with kids—has gone ahead of a slower child and parent, insist that the whole group should assemble at any fork in the trail or major point, like the top of a ridge or a pass, before they continue.

Children should also be told never to throw or roll rocks down a hill toward the trail below; hikers coming up the trail could be seriously injured by their little game.

When the child first begins to walk by herself, the trail itself is enough to absorb her interest. Most trails were never intended for such short legs. But as the child develops confidence and as the trail loses its novelty, she begins to get bored with the hike. This is the point where parents must exercise all their patience and ingenuity to keep everyone going.

THINGS TO TALK ABOUT

Ellyn described their family hikes this way: "We talk and talk and talk." In the beginning, she found that her children didn't really understand why they were hiking. They were not very observant about the environment. They went along with their parents, but their attitude seemed to be, "Why are we doing this?"

Now when they hike, Ellyn and Jon make a special effort to point out to their children all the little things that they themselves enjoy. They stop at cleared spaces to look back at the trail they have just come over and look ahead to see where they are going. They talk about a rockslide, if they pass one, the meadows, what makes a cloud, why is a lake. They talk about their destination and how they will set up their camp.

Families talk about the trail too. Sometimes, when they are hiking in areas that allow it, the children carry bags for picking up "treasures" along the way. Good parents teach their children not to take anything like a flower that is living, or an artifact that is a relic of days gone by. They collect only rocks and sticks and blossoms that have already dropped. When they get to camp or when they stop for lunch, the children take out the things they have gathered and arrange them in a "museum" where everyone can admire them. Then when they go on, they scatter the museum and leave it behind. (I had a discussion with Larry Lang, ranger at Olympic National Park, about the ethics of allowing children to collect "treasures" along the trail or in camp. If we were going to follow park regulations to the letter, he said, then collecting was wrong; however, it would be a terrible thing if the park service stifled children's curiosity. That was not a purpose for which the parks were established, he said, and he saw no problem with children collecting as long as they did not take their treasures home.)

Parents should try to be positive. It's best not to comment to the child about her hiking. If you talk about other things, the child forgets how hard she may be working.

SONGS TO SING

Singing helps the miles go by. Even babies who can't talk enjoy hearing the rest of the family sing. Children love songs that go on and on and on. Everyone soon learns the words to such favorites as "The Ants Go Marching One by One," "Row, Row, Row Your Boat," "This Old Man, He Played One," "Ten Miles from Home," "I Know An Old Lady Who Swallowed A Fly," "Old MacDonald Had a Farm," "Ten Dogs in Bed," "Ninety-nine Bottles of Beer on a Wall," and "Found a Peanut." A Boy Scout or Camp Fire Girl or Boy can teach you all the hiking songs you'd care to know. If your children attend nursery or go to day care, they may know other songs which they can teach you.

Children also like songs about themselves. Our family made up verses for each person in the party to the tune of "The

Quartermaster Corps." We sang,
>"It's Judy, Judy, Judy,
>Who tastes like Tutti-fruitti,
>In the corps, in the corps...."

On one hike, they also had "Jeff, who's going to make us deaf;" "Nancy, who really strikes our fancy;" and (this isn't easy to sing) "John, of whom we all are fond." The verses don't have to make a lot of sense as long as the names are right.

STORY TELLING

Telling stories is another good way to keep the family moving. Most children can never have too much of old favorites like "The Three Little Pigs" and "Goldilocks and The Three Bears." Older children can help move the story along by taking a turn at telling it. If your young child is very impressionable, save the scary stories about sasquatches who live in the woods for a night when you aren't sleeping out. And don't allow an older sibling to tell a ghost story!

The area that you are visiting can be the subject for lots of made-up stories. Make up a story character of your own, like Charlie Chipmunk or Marmeduke Marmot, to talk about only on hikes. Clouds, trees, valleys, rock formations, and mountains are good springboards for the imagination. It doesn't have to be all your own imagination. Let everyone in the family take turns adding to the story. Some families act out familiar stories: "I'm the big, bad wolf and I'm going to find the pig's house of straw."

A story can be an incentive, too. It isn't very practical to start a story at the bottom of a series of steep switchbacks, but if you say, "When we get to the top we'll rest and I'll tell you a story," the child might go up more willingly.

GAMES

The games people play on the trail are those that children are already familiar with, such as "Follow the Leader," "I Spy," "Twenty Questions," or "I Went to Town to Buy an Apple, a Broom," and so on through the alphabet.

Younger children will need to have these games tailored to their abilities. If they don't know the alphabet, they can't play a game that requires them to remember an alphabetical list. Some parents make up a simple naming game that their children enjoy. One five-year-old girl amuses herself by naming as many different kinds of candy as she can think of. Her game could provide hours of fun on a trail if the family took turns naming cars, dogs, flowers, or other objects within a class. If might be wise to avoid naming vegetables or other foods if everyone is hungry.

Rhyming words is another game that can be played while hiking. Everyone in turn must think of a word to rhyme with the chosen word. The last person to think of a word gets to choose the next word to be rhymed. Words that start with a chosen sound are a variation of the same game.

Sammy, who loves to hear about all kinds of animals, plays "Name the Animal" game; his dad names an animal—red fox, velociraptor, bald eagle— and then Sammy walks like that animal. Sammy's dad likes that game because it keeps Sammy close by.

Children who enjoy counting will happily count their steps, or the rocks they pass, or simply count for the fun of it. Older children sometimes like to see how high they can count. Counters-to-one-hundred will repeat themselves many times. Sarah made up a game of "counting noses;" she thought a certain fungus protruding from the sides of some of the trees looked liked noses, and her family not only counted them, but also had a good time pointing to this funny nose or that great big nose.

Any game that can be played without props or score cards is a good game for the trail. Most of these games are also useful for the long trip home in the car. Your local library is a good source of references for starting a collection of games.

REST STOPS

All parents who hike with small children agree that rest stops must be frequent. Some parents say they like to stop before the children get tired. Others use a 15-minute rest for each hour on the trail.

The most important function of a rest stop is the *rest*. If the child is running around while her parents sit, she isn't resting. On the other hand, the child who is carried all the time should be taken out of the carrier and allowed to crawl around and stretch her legs when her parents stop.

Be sure that everyone has a comfortable place to sit or even lie down when you stop. Pull out your windbreakers and sweaters; you'll need them as you cool off. If the ground is damp, get out a poncho or a ground cloth to sit on. Lay a pack on the ground with the top flap stretched out to make a perfect dry seat, with a backrest, for a child.

Now is the time to let your child eat the snacks she has carried in her pocket all day. It's your chance to change the baby's diaper, switch packs, take your toddler to the bathroom in the bushes, and check the children for sunburn and for blisters.

Rest stops can be taken whenever you encounter something interesting. Be on the lookout for trees growing in funny shapes, unusual rocks, a sunny spot on a cool day, a patch of shade when it's hot. Learn to recognize the natural features and the rocks and plants of the area you hike in so you can talk to your children about them. That doesn't mean you have to memorize the name of every flower in the meadow, but if someone in your party is carrying a book about wildflowers, at least some flowers can be identified.

At a rest stop, encourage the children to be so still and

Child sits on open flap of pack to avoid dampness

Don Silverman

quiet that you can hear all the birds. What's that sound? Is it the wind, or a stream or a waterfall? Watch for small animals to creep out. Turn over a rock to see what might be living beneath it—but be sure to turn it back so you don't destroy some creature's home. If you're near a rockslide that might be home to a marmot or a pika, see if you can whistle out one of these friendly, furry animals.

NAPS

A rest stop is not the same thing as a nap. Though all parents agree that rests are a necessity on a hike, most give up on trying to get their kids to take a real honest-to-goodness-lie-down-and-fall-asleep nap. Even those children who nap regularly at home are usually too excited to sleep during the day on a hiking trip. Their parents make up for the lack of sleep by putting the kids to bed at night extra early. They also try to make their lunch stop a time for a good long rest.

The child who rides in a carrier is an exception. There's something about bouncing along in a comfortable bag, close to a warm parent, that must have a lullaby effect on a child. Children who are carried often drop off to sleep and doze away the whole time their parents are hiking; then, when the parents stop to rest, the baby is alert and active and eager to crawl off exploring!

A few parents report that they plan their hikes so that they reach their campsite at midday; they have lunch at the new camp and put their kids down for a nap there. This leaves the afternoon free for the parents. But if your children won't nap, you will find that you have pushed hard to get to your destination early, only to face a long, long afternoon of entertaining the kids.

OTHER GOOD IDEAS FOR THE TRAIL

A child is never too young to learn to be a good trail user. Older children can be taught trail maintenance: improving cross-trail drainage, blocking off incipient shortcuts, tossing fallen branches off trail, and removing rocks from the trail, perhaps placing them along the outer edges of the trail. Picking up litter keeps a young child busy and teaches him service to others at the same time. Some parents make a game of picking up trash, giving a prize—an extra Lifesaver, a handful of raisins—to the child who picks up the most.

The family who buys a year's supply of Valentine candy hearts as their snack food has a built-in incentive to keep their child going. When they pass a one-mile marker, their son gets one heart; at the two-mile marker, two hearts, and so on. Sometimes at the end of a very steep climb he gets one heart of each color. When he finds the sign marking a trail junction, he gets more hearts. As the family think of other goals along the way, they reward him with more candy hearts. Other families can play their games with M & M's or other snacks. In a 1990s version of this game, the Williamses call their snacks "power pills," copying a video game that uses that term to describe a burst of strength.

Giving a child a pack of his own can also be an inducement to happier hiking. A new pack with something important inside will likely be carried without complaining. The child's own sweater or extra clothing won't do; it must be something really important, like lunch for the whole family or all the snacks for rest stops. The child who can say to her older siblings, "You'd better wait for me because I have the lunch," is less likely to complain about the trail. As she grows older she can be given a flashlight, a compass, or—ultimate glory—a knife of her own to carry.

COPING IN CAMP

At last you've made it. After hours on the trail, the last switchback has been climbed, the last song sung, the snack snuck! You've reached your destination and you're ready to make camp. There's lots of work to be done, and if your young children are going to help, the jobs will take longer to do than if you did them yourself. On the other hand, the children will need things to occupy themselves with in camp and they must be constantly watched—no one has childproofed your campsite. What have other parents learned about coping with their children once they get to camp?

SETTING UP LIMITS

Agood way to begin to set up a camp with children is to establish very clear rules about where the children may and may not go. If your children are reasonable kids, you can explain to them why they may not go out of sight; if they haven't yet reached the age of reason, simply tell them quite firmly where to stop. Some parents walk the circuit of the acceptable boundaries with the children so there is no question of how far they may go. If there are other campers in the area, be sure your kids understand that they should not run through their campsite or make a lot of noise in their area.

121

Younger children and kids who just won't stay within limits must be watched all the time. One of the adults must accept the responsibility of watching while the other puts up the tent or cooks; the dangers are too great to allow a child to wander off. Parents who carry a harness or an extra rope find that such a device comes in handy when they must be occupied with setting up camp. This is the time when Beth plays "the elephant game" with her toddler. She ties a short rope to her belt, and gives the other end to Rachel, who follows her mom around camp just the way elephants on parade hold on to one another's tails. Don gets the rope for their food-hanging set up early so his kids can swing on it; a sturdy stick or several knots tied on the end provides a platform. (More about food-hanging later.)

Older children will be allowed more freedom than younger ones, but when there are several children in the family it's easiest to give them all the same limitations. When your children are experienced you can say to them, as one mother does, "Play where you can see us." Even so, she spends more time keeping track of her children than her children spend looking at her.

Some parents who carry whistles for emergencies don't use them on the trail, when their kids must stay close, but they get them out in camp, where the children are freer. But don't depend too much on a whistle. Anita reported a frightening half-hour she spent at twilight looking for two nine-year-olds who had taken a walk along a beautiful stream. The rushing water drowned out all sound. She shouted and whistled, but they couldn't hear her. Until they saw her waving a flashlight, they had no idea that she was looking for them.

CHORES

In many families the children are not free to play until the camp is set up. Everyone has an assignment that he must do to make the campsite home for the night. Other families give the kids a free time when they first arrive in camp, as a break from the discipline of hiking, and assign chores later. Most parents find that children are quite enthusiastic about having an important job, and in camp all jobs are important.

If you're camping in an area where fires are permitted, even very small children can go along with an adult and help gather wood for a fire. Don't expect to keep a fire going very long with just the wood your little one brings in, but be sure to recognize this contribution.

Other chores include helping a parent carry water, if he's a toddler, or getting it himself if he's old enough and there's no risk, like falling into a stream. Holding the outlet hose while an adult pumps the water filter is a very responsible job for a small child. All children can help clear away the sticks and stones that may break your bones if they're under your tent floor. Helping to set up the tent isn't work at all, it's fun, especially if you get to crawl inside the deflated tent and hold up a pole. Children can also help spread out the insulating pads that you sleep on and they can lay out their own sleeping bags.

Kitchen work provides great opportunities for children. Young children should not cook over a wood fire or even over a stove, which may be tippy, but they are great shakers and stirrers. If there is gelatin, pudding, or fruit drink to be prepared, they can do it almost by themselves.

Cleaning up is another good chore time. Children can scrape dishes before they are washed and assist with the rinsing and drying. Julie took over the dishwashing assignment in her family and did them all by herself, washing them in one pot and rinsing them in another. Her mother waited until she was asleep before washing them again—she did not want to ruin her daughter's pleasure the first time around. Children can also carry the

Helping Daddy carry heavy bucket

Thomas Winnett

Don Silverman

One child helps with tent while other rides on Dad

dishwater away from camp and away from stream or lake to a designated spot and dump it.

A few children are not enthusiastic about camp chores. Here again every parent must know his own child. If the trip is supposed to be fun for everyone, don't force a reluctant child to do more than a minimum amount of work as his contribution to the family's outing.

GAMES AND PLAY

Actually the work of camping takes up very little of a child's time. Most of the time he spends in camp he will be free to play. It helps sometimes if parents have suggestions to give a child when he asks, "What shall I do now?" However, parents don't need to fill every minute with something to do. Children are remarkable creatures; they find all sorts of ways to amuse themselves, and sometimes they like just to daydream, doing nothing at all.

A young baby is a "looker." He may be content to stay in his backpack propped against a tree and watch the activity of setting up camp. Later he can be moved to a ground cloth where he has kicking room. A crawling baby might also be willing to stay in the baby carrier for a short time, if you're lucky, while you set up the tent. It helps sometimes if he has something to handle, and for this your pack is full of goodies. Spoons, cups, a bright bandanna, a pan with a lid, some clothes pins—any of these in addition to the rattle or teething biscuits you brought will keep him busy while you work. A baby can also play safely in a zipped-up tent, a good place to put him for a short time if you need a 10-minute break or if the mosquitoes in camp are annoying.

Toddlers like doing things, and again your equipment offers many opportunities. Filling and emptying doesn't require a fancy bucket and shovel; it's just as much fun with a cup and a spoon. Piling up is another game from the pack. In fact, the pack itself can amuse a child for hours, with filling, emptying, and zippering. A hiking boot is just as challenging to unlace as one of those bright wooden shoes you buy in a toy store.

Water is fun if it's a warm day and you have a safe spot. Filling and emptying again, tossing rocks to make a splash, launching sticks or leaves in a stream, digging in sand or mud— the possibilities go on and on. A parent who can skip a rock has a chance to show off, and an older child may learn to skip a rock himself. "Pooh sticks" is a common water game; players toss their stick into a stream on one side of a footbridge, a log, or some other barrier, and then run to the other side to see whose stick arrives first. A broad leaf threaded on a thin twig and jammed into a piece of bark makes a fine biodegradable sailboat.

Pre-schoolers can play all these games and more. They can draw pictures on the ground; make collages of leaves, stones, and sticks imbedded in mud; or make hand puppets out of plastic bags and rubber bands from the pack. With a small car or two from his pack, a child can create a system of roads on the ground, leading to a town or a farm. Sometimes he won't need the cars; a rock or a piece of wood will do.

Older children like to play Fort or Spying. Or they may be ready for simple lessons in holding a knife to make shavings or in striking a match properly. They might bring along a tiny deck of cards for "Old Maid" or "Crazy Eights." And a piece of string is all it takes to play "Cat's Cradle."

On a camping trip the whole family can play together. Your child may love playing the old games of "London Bridge" or "Ring Around the Rosy" with you. Avoid "Hide and Seek" if you're in a heavily wooded area; it's potentially dangerous. Try instead a caterpillar or a slug race, where members of the family vie to see whose caterpillar will be first to crawl out of a circle drawn on the ground. Be sure to return your caterpillars to the greenery they were found in when you are through.

Quieter games for sitting around the campfire or just sitting include all the guessing games you used on the trail. There's also a whispering game called "Gossip" or "Telephone," in which you send a message around a circle to see how garbled it gets. The Asian game of "Rock, Paper, Scissors" amuses some children for hours.

Here are some games that may be new to your family. The first one is called "Chinese Numbers." Arrange some twigs or blades of grass in a pattern and then rest your hands in front of you. Ask your audience to "guess what number it is." Rearrange the twigs and ask them again. Finally you divulge that the pattern of the twigs doesn't matter at all; the correct number is determined by the number of fingers you are showing on your hands. Once the children learn this game, they can be the "sayers" and an indulgent parent can be the person who tries to guess the number.

"Huckle, Buckle, Beanstalk" is a game in which some object—a compass or a band-aid, say—is left out in a visible but not obvious place. The players walk around looking for it. The first person who sees it sits down and says, "Huckle, buckle, beanstalk," and waits for the others to find it. It's important not to stare at the object and give away its location. When everyone has spotted it, the first person who saw it gets to hide it while the others close their eyes.

In one family, the favorite quiet game is camp checkers. Someone draws a "board" in the dirt that's eight by eight squares. Then they search for flat black and white rocks, twelve of each, to use as "checkers." Setting up this game is sometimes more fun than playing it!

Gathering, cooking, and eating wild foods is an activity the whole family can share. If that sounds too ambitious, try berry picking: "one for the bucket and one for me." Be sure everyone understands which berries are edible. Or you can find and name wildflowers; don't pick them, just find them. There are good books on these subjects, many of them lightweight enough to go along in a pack. If the flowers are too beautiful just to leave, try sketching or photographing them. A seven-year-old can handle a simple camera, though his idea of a good subject may be something other than wildflowers!

Another family activity involves the sounds of camp. Most of the sounds you hear are new and strange, and are hard to identify. Tracing a sound to its source is a safe adventure, as long as a careful parent goes with the children. Surprisingly, there are many, many different sounds in your quiet camp if you really stop to listen.

Lessons in identifying rocks and birds are interesting to some children. Collecting fallen specimens for a museum is just as easy in camp as it was on the trail. A small magnifying glass for looking at things around camp may provide hours of pleasure. Don't pull it out until you get to camp; if you take it out on the trail, you may never get to camp.

If one of the grown-ups in your party has a special outdoor activity, let the whole family participate. If it's fishing, let everyone fish. Older children can learn real fishing techniques, but the younger ones will be just as happy dragging the water with a stick, a string, and a makeshift "fis" of some sort—a twig or a leaf will do.

There's a father in our area whose pack is full of odds and ends of ropes. He learned lashing when he was a boy, and when his family sets up a camp, they furnish it beautifully with racks and tables made of fallen branches lashed together. When they're ready to leave they simply untie all the furniture and take their ropes home.

EATING

Eating in camp is not difficult; feeding is what's hard. The only problem that arises, usually, with the child who can feed himself is providing enough to satisfy his big outdoor appetite. Even fussy eaters are sometimes so hungry they "forget" that they don't like noodles! But the child who is spoonfed at home is a little more difficult to handle in camp.

Some parents feed their one-year-olds in the baby carrier. They strap the child in, prop him against a tree (if the carrier doesn't have its own support), and spoon away. A clean diaper or bandanna draped around the carrier protects it from flying baby food. And here's a happy thought as he knocks that spoonful of oatmeal from your hand: there's no floor or wall to scrub out there.

Don Silverman

"Don't worry, girls — there's enough for everyone."

Other parents report that they have better luck when they hold the child in one arm and feed him with the other hand. With one of the baby's arms immobilized between the child's body and the parent's, and the other arm held by the parent's encircling arm, the baby can't send his food out to the wild blue yonder.

Using a third technique, one parent holds the baby on her lap with the arms pinned down, while the other parent spoons the food in as fast as he can. This method assumes that both parents are available to feed the baby. It was suggested by the parents of one, and might not work in a family that had an infant *and* a three-year-old.

What a commotion just to feed such a tiny person! It's a relief to settle down afterward and lean against a comfortable rock or tree trunk while you give the baby his bottle or let him nurse.

If parents aren't fussy about manners, older children have no trouble spooning their dinners from cup to mouth. A plate is a little harder to manage because it has no handle to hold onto. It's a long way up to your mouth from your lap. It helps to seat a child next to a makeshift table of some sort—a stump or a flat rock. Then his food has less distance to travel. Menus planned with lots of finger foods are easiest for the child who is just learning to use a fork and spoon.

If your child is not very skillful at feeding himself but too proud to be fed, try to improvise a table that he can get right up to. Set up two rocks, logs, or packs, and lay across them a flat piece of wood or several thin branches, so that the child sitting cross-legged on the ground has a platform to sit at.

Toddlers whose shirt fronts catch a lot of falling food should wear plastic bibs while they eat. You don't have to tell them it's a bib; call it a camper's apron or a chest protector.

Most adult backpackers fill their plates at the cookstove and walk off to find a comfortable place to eat. Young backpackers shouldn't be expected to do the same. Very few children can carry a full plate or cup over uneven ground without spilling. If a child makes it to where he's going, he's sure to spill in the process of sitting down. Experienced parents seat their children first and then bring the filled plates or cups to them.

TOILETING

"**B**ut, Mommy, where's the bathroom?"

What do children find when they look for the bathroom in the woods?

Where the park or forest management has provided it, there will be an outhouse with a "one-holer" inside. In other locations they will find just the box with the hole and no house around it. Often there are lots of flies and a bad smell. The deep hole in the ground that all the kids look into is really scary. Little wonder that many children balk completely at using these facilities. Many parents feel the same way. Adults can overcome their revulsion. With children it's easier to take them into the woods and teach them how to go about toileting there, just as if there were no boxes available.

The rules for toileting in the wilderness seem simple enough. Choose a place that is away from the trail, far from any lake or stream, so that you don't contaminate the water. (In camp you should designate as the bathroom an area some distance away from your tent site and every other possible campsite.) There you dig a little hole, a "cat hole," with the lightweight trowel you're carrying for just that purpose, or with a stick or the heel of your boot. It should be 4" to 6" deep. Squat over the hole, deposit body wastes in it, and cover it all up well. Drop your toilet paper into a plastic bag. There should be at least two inches of soil covering the deposit. Some families dig a short trench for all to use, starting at one end of the trench and covering it gradually during their stay at that camp-site.

Over a period of time and in the presence of heat and water, microorganisms living in the top six inches of soil will break down the buried matter into innocuous elements. The process is called *biodegradation,* and any product capable of being broken down that way is called *biodegradable.* Because the paper decomposes more slowly than fecal material, hikers should bury just their body wastes and carry the toilet paper out with their garbage.

All these instructions hold true even if you are using biodegradable toilet paper. You already know not to bury the foil wrapper and the moist towelette that you used on your hands when you were finished, because they are not biodegradable. But even the most biodegradable paper won't break down in soil unless heat and moisture are also present. Consider the stories you've heard about artifacts that lasted for years and years after they were abandoned in the desert or in arctic lands. That's why backpackers traveling over snowfields or in the desert should follow different instructions.

Where fecal material won't decompose, it should be carried out. Just as many communities have "scooper" laws that require dog owners to clean up after their pets, hikers on permanent snowfields should plan to carry out their own feces. Use your lightweight trowel to scoop wastes into small doubled plastic bags; or put the bags over your hand, grasp the feces, and then turn the bag inside out. Drop toilet paper in the same bag.

In the desert, you might expect the dry air to take care of body wastes. I talked to Dan Johnson, a ranger at Olympic National Park, who had also worked in the southwestern parks. He told me they had tried for several years a "smear" technique, thinking that feces smeared on the hot and barren ground would quickly dry up and blow away; it didn't happen. He recommends that feces and paper should both be carried out. However, campers who object to doing that could bury their wastes and burn their paper in an empty can that is carried just for that purpose. Be sure that all the paper is consumed and the ashes are cold before you leave them; better still, carry them out with your garbage. Don't burn the paper unless you have a can; in Washington state in 1985, a group of campers trying to practice minimum-impact camping burned their toilet paper and started a fire that destroyed half a million dollars worth of forest.

In a healthy person, urine is sterile, so contaminating the water supply is not the problem when choosing a place to pee; rather, it is the distinct and disagreeable odor that lingers where many people have relieved themselves. In areas that have a lot of rainfall, like the Pacific Northwest, dilution should take care of the odor. In very arid areas like Grand Canyon National Park, where there is no possibility of dilution, we were instructed to pee in the river when we were near it; otherwise, we were told to look for "wet sand." In Olympic National Park we were told to pee on the trail, where the soil is already impacted and sterile. A different problem arises in that park; the deer, attracted to the salt left on the underbrush by dried urine, will chew it down to the ground.

These subtle distinctions would be lost on most children; for them, the cat hole for all toileting makes the best sense. For further information on the impact of many people descending on the wilderness and leaving their wastes behind, Ranger Johnson recommended a book that has the unfortunate title of *How to Shit in the Woods*, by Kathleen Meyer, Ten Speed Press.

Children who begin backpacking as infants and continue to hike regularly with their parents have no difficulties, usually, adjusting to toileting in the outdoors. But other children—those who don't hike often and those who make their first trip at the age of four—often have problems accepting outdoor facilities. You can understand their dilemma; these little people have only recently learned to inhibit their bowel and bladder. Now they are being asked to relax that hard-learned control in new, strange situations and in a new position. It's no wonder some of them have problems.

Squatting as such is not a difficult position for children; many can squat and play for hours. What seems to be difficult for some children is relaxing the sphincters enough to urinate or defecate in that position. What can parents do to help a child who obviously needs to relieve himself but is just too tense to let go?

To begin with, the child should be as comfortable as possible. Make sure that the place where he is squatting is level and that there is no underbrush in his face or at his back. Don't hurry the child; assure him that you have all the time in the world. Sometimes it helps if only one parent stays with the child; certainly no brothers and sisters should be waiting around impatiently. Talk to him quietly, and praise him when finally he is able to produce.

The mother (or father) who stays with the child should

be comfortable too. Otherwise she might inadvertently give the child the impression that she is trying to hurry him, and that will make him more tense. Unless you have unusual stamina, that means you shouldn't try to squat as long as the child can. Seat yourself comfortably on a log or a rock or the ground, and be prepared to wait patiently for as long as it may take.

Parents should watch their children while they're hiking and be aware of when the youngsters last went to the bathroom. Sometimes a child is so leery of a strange situation that he may try to "hold it" rather than admit he needs to stop. One little boy kept saying that he felt cold; his mother now understands that he gets a little chill when he has to have a bowel movement.

There are many things parents can do to help their children defecate. Time of day is an important factor. Try to arrange your day so that the child is free and relaxed at approximately the same time as he has his bowel movement at home. Give him something to eat just beforehand to set the digestive process in motion. Watch his diet; if he has hard stools, let him snack on raisins, dates, and prunes, but keep him away from nuts and soybeans.

Some children who are particularly tense or who have a tendency toward constipation may go for days unable to produce a bowel movement while squatting. One little girl's parents solved her problem by creating a "throne" for their child. They placed two flat-topped rocks close together but not touching, and dug out the dirt between them. The girl sat on the rocks while her mother told her a story, and soon she was able to fill the hole.

Another family carries a child's plastic toilet seat with them when they hike. Their little girl was accustomed to using a lightweight seat without back or arms that simply fit into the larger seat at home. After several unhappy tiffs about squatting, they decided to carry the seat along. The seat rests between two rocks or logs—a more luxurious throne that the first girl's, and just as effective. She calls it "the bears' potty."

The "bear's potty"

The discussion of toileting so far might seem to indicate that producing bowel movements is the only problem. Actually little girls, and boys who have not yet learned to urinate while standing, often have as much trouble urinating in the squatting position as they do defecating. Many parents have watched their daughters squat dryly for many minutes, only to have them stand up and immediately wet themselves. If parents are calm and patient and willing to try new ways, these children can learn to urinate outdoors too. One little girl who does not like to squat developed her own unusual position. She stands with her legs wide apart, leaning backwards while her parents hold onto her hands. Another girl simply spreads her legs wide apart while standing. As long as the children keep their clothing out of the way, these methods are just fine.

Little girls—and boys who squat to defecate—have special problems managing their clothing. If they haven't gathered their pant legs together tightly or if they have squatted uphill of their clothes, they may stand up and find that their pants are all wet. In rainy weather, they must be taught to drop their pants, but not too far. Otherwise they may spoil all your efforts at keeping them dry by dropping their pants right into a puddle.

Urinating seems never to be a problem for little boys who can stand. In fact, it is often hard to limit them to the area that the family has set aside for toileting; some little boys take great delight in marking off their territorial rights like male wolves by encircling their campsite with a ring of urine. Although such novelty appeals to little boys, parents really should discourage their sons from that activity. Imagine yourselves as the next family to camp at that spot!

A child who is only partly toilet-trained is in a class by himself. One mother labeled this child as the most difficult kind of youngster to take hiking. Your decision on how you will deal with the training situation depends on many variables. For one example, wetting accidents that require a change of clothing are much easier to handle on a day trip than on a three-day outing. For another, a father who had rigged a seat for his daughter in the top compartment of his pack was concerned that she might flood the lower section where their gear was stowed.

The method you are using to train the child will also make a difference. A child who is taken to the bathroom at regular intervals can continue his schedule in the woods. A little boy who is being trained to urinate standing up may actually make greater strides in control when he is encouraged to do so outdoors. On the other hand, the child who is supposed to let his parents know when he has to "go potty" will probably not be very successful out of doors. At first the novelty of going behind a tree may trigger many false alarms; later the new surroundings may make the child forgetful of his own needs until it is too late.

For some parents, trying to maintain training while hiking is just too much work. They put their child back in diapers just for the trip; if the child doesn't object, his progress toward self-control will probably not be set back. On the other hand, if the child feels strongly, as one young lady did, that diapers are for babies and she is a big girl, the parents will just have to pack lots of extra pants and panties and plastic bags and wash cloths and more of that good old patience, humor, and common sense. Just keep reminding yourself, next year won't be like this!

WASHING

A t the same time that your child learns rules of toileting, he should also be taught how to wash afterward. On the trail the child's hands will probably be washed with a premoistened towelette. In camp, especially at bedtime, you can use a basin, a wash cloth, and a small towel for a thorough once-a-day cleaning.

Teach your child to fill a basin with water from a stream or a lake and carry it away from the bank. If you were smart and planned ahead, you will have some water heated on the campfire or the stove waiting to add to your creek water. Wash the child with a soapy corner of the wash cloth, rinse with the other three corners, and dry him with the towel. When you are finished, dump the water on the ground far from any lake or stream.

Washing your children and washing their clothes in camp are really much the same. Teach your child to do all the washing in the basin, not in a stream or a lake. Even if you use biodegradable soap, the dirt you wash off your hands or clothes is a pollutant. And in a cold mountain creek, the process of breaking down your soap will take a long, long time. Would you want to camp downstream from your dirty laundry?

BEDTIME

Among the most precious moments for parents on a hiking trip is that shared time when the kids are asleep in the tent and you finally have a chance to relax and talk to each other. But before that, if you want to have a peaceful night, there are certain jobs that have to be done.

If bears visit the camps in your area, or if you want to discourage rodents from nibbling at your pack, you must put all your food out of reach. If you didn't do it earlier, choosing a tree to hang the food on is task that you can assign to your older children after supper. To foil bears, the food bag must be at least 12 feet up and 10 feet out from the tree trunk. Finding the right spot could be a real challenge, unless you're camping in an area where the managers have provided a bar high enough off the ground, like the goal-post crossbar on a football field, for hanging food.

Remove all food from the tent, and check your children's pockets to be sure they don't have a few peanuts or a candy wrapper hidden away. Animals have a very strong sense of smell. Gather all the food and your garbage into one big sack; the stuff bag that their tent traveled in is the bag that many families use. Tie two metal cups to the outside of the bag that will clink and alert you if a bear should disturb them. Then tie a weight— small rock will do— to the end of a length of lightweight nylon line (1/8th inch or so in diameter), and hurl it up and over the branch you have chosen. It may take more than one trial. Tie the lightweight rope to a heavier rope and pull it over the branch. Tie that heavier rope to the food bag and haul it up out of reach. Wrap the other end of the rope around the trunk of the tree several times, or around a nearby tree if it's handier, and knot it.

If you can't find a branch in the right place that is strong enough to hold your food bag, you will have to use the same rock-throwing technique to hang a rope between two trees, and then suspend your food from the center of that rope

Some hikers carry a small block and tackle to "tree" their food bag, and others carry a mountaineer's carabiner. They pass the heavier rope through the hardware of their choice, and haul it up onto the branch with the lightweight rope. Then it's much easier to pull the food bag up, and the rope is less likely to snag on some bark.

In the Campmor catalogue, I found a bear bag, a stuff sack with sewn-in webbing loops, 40 feet of cord, and an attached rock sack. You put the rock in the sack to throw it over the branch. When I saw this I thought, why have I spent so many years trying to tie up a rock? I could have been carrying my own small rock sack!

The counter-balance method is another way to hang your bag. Throw the lightweight line over the branch as above.

Pulling the food bag up onto the tree

When you have the line over the branch, tie a rock or a piece of fallen wood that weighs about the same as your bag of food to one end of the line. (Instead of a rock, you could tie a bag containing half the food, if you have two appropriate bags.) Now pull the rock up to the branch that the line passes over. Then tie your food bag to the other end of the line, as high as you can conveniently reach, and stuff any extra line into the mouth of the food bag. Now push up on the food bag with just enough force—you hope—that the system will come to rest with the rock and the bag equally high. If they aren't equally high, take a long enough stick, preferably forked, and push up the lower of the two until they are even. If a 6-foot person could reach them standing on tiptoes, they are too low. Try again. Next morning, push up either rock or bag until one descends enough that you can reach it.

Bears who have been introduced to "people food" through carelessness with garbage and through tourists who actually feed them have become a problem in many areas. In these places and in areas where there are no trees, authorities recommend bear-resistant food containers. These high-impact plastic canisters are opened with a coin or a screw driver—another item to add to your backpacking necessities list. In the Sierras, they tell me bear canisters will soon be required. Only one park in Washington state, North Cascades National Park, requires bear canisters, and then only in certain areas; the canisters are rented with a credit card, and if they are not returned, a charge goes through. In Mount Rainier National Park, bears are not a problem. In Olympic National Park, buckets with snap-on lids are required in the coastal camping areas because of problems with raccoons. Some campgounds were closed in the summer of 1998 because of a sudden rash of bear problems. A ranger told me that in some places where bears are a problem, the park management has installed bear-proof lockers at designated campsites. Bear canisters are available through REI and Campmor, which also sells a nylon carrying case so the canister can be tied to a pack. (See Appendix B) The canisters weigh about 2½ pounds, and they are not inexpensive, more good reasons for checking beforehand with the authorities in the area where you will be going. In the High Sierra of California, some rangers say nothing works except 1) bear boxes permanently installed by authorities in popular camping areas, and 2) canisters carried by the backpackers themselves.

Before the children are tucked away in their sleeping bags, each one should be taken to your toileting area to be sure his or her bladder is emptied. Dress them in their night clothes or undress them down to a semiclean sleeping layer. Those who wear diapers should be pinned up with extra thicknesses; even a 5-year-old can sometimes be persuaded to wear a diaper to protect the sleeping bag from possible accidents. Be careful! Changing a diaper in a tent can surprise you unless you're prepared for it. Baby boys should be kept covered at all times. A father who left his son uncovered for a moment as he turned aside for a fresh diaper was caught by a sudden fountain of urine which shot straight up, deflected off the top of the tent, and soaked the two of them.

While the kids are still awake, gather and arrange in a handy place all the things you might possibly need during the night and all the things you will need first thing in the morning. You should include diapers, a bottle or a canteen of water, a flashlight, toilet paper, paper tissues, and anything else your family may require. Then get out the clothes you plan to sleep in and place them where you can easily find them.

Arrange the children in their assigned spaces in the tent, sing them a song or tell them a story, and then leave them. One more job and you are free: take a few minutes to police the area outside the tent. Packs that are left out should be covered with plastic bags or tarps to keep the dew off. Clear the path from the tent to the toileting area of any obstacles that you might trip over during the night like tent ropes, rocks, or logs.

Finally comes your own time. Of course, by now you may be so tired that you crawl into bed yourself. Many parents don't stay up later than their children. But if you do stay up, remember when you go to bed you must be very, very quiet. Get into the night clothes that you left out and slip into your sleeping bag without saying a word: if the children wake up now, you may never get them back to sleep. John and Lisa, crawling into their zipped-together bags where their daughter was already asleep, accidentally woke her. She was delighted by the arrival of company, and since she had an hour of sleep behind her, she kept them awake for several hours of play!

WATCH OUT FOR CHILDREN —SAFETY

This chapter is probably the most important chapter in this book.

All of us have read of too many tragedies involving children lost or injured in the outdoors. A concern for safety and accident prevention is vital to any hiking trip with children. Hopefully that attitude has come through in the earlier pages of this book, but the subject is so important that the warnings bear repeating. Therefore, this chapter will reconsider your hiking and camping trip with an emphasis on accident prevention.

DANGERS ON THE TRAIL

Before you leave home, you should inform somebody of where you will be and when you expect to return. Tell this "home guard" that if you do not get back on time, he should call the sheriff or other responsible authority (leave the appropriate phone number) and ask them to see if your car is still at the trailhead. If it is, they should send out a search party. It is very important that you give clear and accurate information. If there is more than one Heather Lake or Lookout Mountain in

Goldie Silverman

Have your child wear a whistle always, and know when to use it—and when not to

your area, be sure the home guard knows which one you are going to. If you have alternate plans in case of bad weather, bad fishing, or other problems that you may not know in advance, tell your home guard about them. When you transmit this information, be certain that the home guard understands what you mean. A family of dayhikers told a neighbor, "We're always out before dark," meaning out of the woods; but the neighbor interpreted their instructions to mean that they would be home before dark, and he spent a frantic evening calling searchers.

Everyone in your hiking party must follow the rules. That can't be emphasized enough. Children should stay on the trail at all times. If they should have to go to the bathroom, an adult should go off the trail with them. Modest children can duck out of sight behind a tree or a bush without leaving their guardian's immediate vicinity.

Older children who are allowed to hike ahead of the family should be severely limited in how far they may go. "Wait at the first switchback," or "Wait at the trail fork," seem to be simple orders to follow—if everyone agrees on what a "fork" and a "switchback" are. Children who repeatedly walk farther ahead than their parents have permitted them to should be kept back with the larger family group, or else one adult in the group should go ahead with them.

All children need to be taught what to do if they should become separated from the group. A lost child, initially, is not far from her family. If the child panics, runs wildly, grows hot and throws off her coat, hears noises that sound to her like scary monsters (when they may actually be searchers shouting), or worries that she will be punished, then she increases her own danger. So teach your children what to do if they think they are lost. Tell them to stay where they are, sit down, keep warm, and signal with their whistle. Assure them in advance that they will be found if they stay in one place and don't wander around. Explain to them that if they hear a noise, they should shout at it; if it's an animal, it will be frightened away, but if it's a searcher, he will bring the child to safety. Let them know that you will not be angry with them. Tell them that, if they should be lost, they have hundreds of friends who will turn out to help look for them; tell them this is one time when it is okay to talk to strangers. Read to them the little book, *Willie Takes a Hike*, by Gloria Rand, illustrated by Ted Rand (Harcourt Brace), to help get these lessons across.

An organization in California called Hug-A-Tree and Survive™ has assembled a slide show to teach grade school children what to do if they are lost; the program is presented by volunteers nationwide. You can contact them at (619) 286-7536 for more information.

Most parents would not deliberately lead their children into a hazardous situation, but sometimes dangers do come along. A washed-out section of a trail, a strange animal, a change of weather can all make a happy trip suddenly unsafe. It is important for adults to remain matter-of-fact about potential peril. If the trail becomes difficult, children should be warned calmly of the risk and shown how to pass the dangerous point safely. A possible problem with animals, insects, or the weather should be approached the same way. Teach the children to cope with these hazards without scaring them so much that the hike is spoiled.

Without frightening the children, instruct them not to pick up strange bugs or snakes. Warn them that most berries are not edible. Tell them that some plants are very irritating to brush up against. Teach them not to go poking around in holes or hollow stumps or logs. Even if there are no dangerous animals inside, harmless creatures should not be tortured. Educate them about bees and wasps; if they can hear buzzing, they should be on the lookout for bees; if a hornet or two brushes against their arm, they should be ready to retreat.

Older children can be reasoned with; indeed, the hazards you encounter can be a springboard to a nature-study lesson. But toddlers should be watched carefully all the time. That same great outdoors that's full of fresh air and healthy activity is also full of pitfalls for inquisitive tots.

Be alert to problems that children may be having. Some children are complainers. They freely communicate to their parents any discomforts they have. Others are silent sufferers. Watch for signs of unhappiness in your child. Blisters, chafing clothing, sunburn, and fatigue should all be dealt with as soon as possible. Be ready to lend a helping hand over rough places and to alter your plans if the trip turns out to be too much for your child. The rare persons who are allergic to the stings of bees and other insects suffer much more severely from bites than ordinary people do; their reactions require immediate emergency treatment. Consult your doctor or nurse before your first trip if you're not up on the proper first-aid treatment of insect bites, sunburn, diarrhea, broken bones, high fever, and other things that might afflict children in the wilderness. Getting up-to-date booster shots against tetanus at the same time is a good idea for both children and parents.

Snacks are not ordinarily risky, but they become potentially unsafe if a child is allowed to eat as she walks along a trail. Most children cannot concentrate on eating and walking at the same time. Dropping the cookie is the least of possible problems. The child who is thinking about her handful of raisins is likely to trip and fall, hurting herself as well as losing her raisins. A child hiking along with a piece of hard candy in her mouth could easily choke on it. A mouthful of any food is a danger while walking, and candy on a stick is particularly perilous.

When you plan your menus for your hiking trips, be sure that the foods you take are age-appropriate for your family. According to surveys conducted by Johns Hopkins University, the following foods were most often involved in fatal choking episodes in children under age five:

> Hot dogs, sausages
> Round candy
> Peanuts, nuts
> Grapes
> Hard cookies, biscuits
> Meat chunks or slices
> Raw carrot slices or sticks
> Peanut butter, peanut-butter sandwiches
> Apple chunks or slices
> Popcorn

All of these are foods you might take with you when you hike. If you do, be sure your children are seated, not walking around, when they eat them. Cut the food into pieces small enough for your child to handle. Don't introduce new solids on this list to your infant on a camping trip.

PROBLEMS WITH THE BABY CARRIER

Parents carrying children in baby carriers must take extra care to prevent accidents. Never bend forward from the waist to retrieve something from the ground; if you must pick up something, bend from the knees. Carry the pack high enough on your back so that the baby's feet will not be injured if you should sit down unexpectedly. Be on guard for low branches that could brush across the baby's face. And never carry a child in a pack unless she is secured by a safety strap.

The child riding in the pack should be checked frequently for signs of chafing or hot spots where her legs have rubbed against the packframe or the fabric between her legs. Lift her out and change her position often to avoid circulation problems from inactivity. Some parents report increased diaper rash in babies who spend the whole day in a carrier; use a protective ointment to prevent this. In cold, wet weather, check frequently to be sure the baby is warm and dry.

Stay off steep snow slopes with a baby in a backpack. For that matter, don't go any place where you might easily fall. Roped climbs are for times when you leave the kids at home.

SAFETY IN CAMP

It is just as important in camp as it is on the trail that everyone understands and follows the rules. Although the limited area of your site lessens some potential dangers, the greater freedom your child has there increases other hazards.

Children should be told to stay within the camp boundaries at all times. However, if your child should wander off, she must know what to do. This is a lesson that requires great tact from parents. On the one hand, the child is told that she must stay in camp, and on the other hand she is told what to do when she doesn't stay in camp. The same rules for getting found (after you have gotten lost) that you taught on the trail apply in camp. A story is another way to get the lesson across:

"Once upon a time, there was a little girl (or boy) who walked away from her tent and got lost. So she sat down on the ground and waited for her parents. She waited and she waited. Pretty soon her parents found her and they all lived happily ever after." Of course your story can be embellished with many more exciting details, about hearing noises and shouting or blowing her whistle.

If you hike in an area where campfires are still allowed, the fire is probably the greatest danger within your camp. An open fire must be guarded at all times. Children should not be allowed to cook over the fire or to put things into it. Toddlers should not walk along the borders of the fire pit where they might fall into it. Older sisters and mothers with long hair should have their hair tied back whenever they work near the fire.

Clothing should be checked to see whether it's flammable. Loose clothing—a flowing nightgown or a floppy, open shirt—is more likely to catch fire than snug, fitted garments. Wool is very slow to catch fire and to burn; cotton is just the opposite, quick to catch and burn. Polyester and nylon are slower than cotton, but not as slow as wool. Most fleece is made of polyester, but some, especially the kind used for sweatshirts, may be made of cotton; read the labels carefully. The underwear ads in the L.L.Kids Catalog warn that both their cotton and polyester garments are "Not intended for use as sleepwear." That's not to say the kids can't sleep in their underwear, only that there are much more stringent rules on flammability for children's sleepwear than for daytime clothing. Some manufacturers of disposable diapers have voluntarily placed the following warning on their packages: "Diapers will burn if exposed to flame. Keep your child away from any source of flame."

Put the stove where a child can't reach it

Goldie Silverman

Even the backpacker's stove can be a risk if a youngster gets too close to it. Put your stove up on a rock or a stump where a curious crawler can't reach up and pull it over on himself. Keep your fuel containers and fire starters out of reach of your little ones.

Watch the things that your baby plays with. Before you let her attack your pack, remove all the unsafe things like the stove, fuel, and first-aid items.

Check your campsite for poisonous plants, especially berries and mushrooms, and keep your youngsters away from them.

Moving out from your campsite, what possible pitfalls in the neighborhood might attract your children? A cliff is doubly dangerous. You know about the chance of falling from the top, but even the base may not be a safe place to play. Crumbly clay cliffs or loose dirt banks can give way where children dig or climb on them. Children have been caught and buried in such earth slides. Rocky slopes are fun to cross, but you must be on the lookout for loose boulders. An adult can start a rock rolling that might injure or crush a child climbing below him.

Dry streambeds are unsafe in some parts of the country; a cloudburst miles away can send a wall of water crashing down the streambed. In some areas, water released from a dam or water due to heavy rainfall in the mountains causes rapid rising downstream.

Campers at a beach have special perils to watch for. For one thing, if you didn't consult a tide table, the incoming tide may catch you and leave you stranded. Logs are another risk. Don't allow your children to climb on logs at the water's edge; the next wave may roll the log, topple your child off, and pin her underneath. Wave-floated logs may bump an unwary person and break a leg. Insecure logs balanced across others at the upper edge of the beach may shift and crush a careless climber.

Do these stories sound like scare tactics from an overly protective grandmother? Each one is based on a true accident that happened to real children. You don't need to become immobilized with fear, only be alert to the special attractiveness to children of these and other hazards you probably already know about.

HAZARDS FROM WEATHER

A forecast of steady rain is a good reason for postponing a trip and staying home. If a sudden shower catches you on the trail, ponchos can protect the children. In camp the kids may be content to play inside the tent until the shower is over. But if the children get wet, it's important to get them warm and dry as soon as possible.

When young hikers get cold and wet, their parents should be watchful for signs of *hypothermia*, a condition of low body temperature brought on by chilling that cools the body faster than it can generate heat. Symptoms include shivering, slurred speech, unsteady gait, irrational behavior, and of course low temperature. It is particularly difficult to diagnose in small children since so many of the symptoms are part of normal behavior in the average two-year-old. Hypothermia is treated by warming the victim: give warm fluids to drink and put her in a heated bed or in a sleeping bag with another person to provide body warmth.

Hypothermia is easier to avoid than it is to treat. In cool weather, or when it's wet or windy, keep the children warm and dry with proper clothing and hats. Offer them warm drinks periodically. Keep the kids moving; avoid long lunch stops in the cold. When you do stop, get out of the wind. The child riding in a carrier will need extra layers of clothing because she isn't generating heat through exercise. A windproof outer layer will help

Sunblock and a hat for parent and child

Thomas Winnett

prevent the loss of body heat. Keeping the child in the carrier close to her parent's body will also help keep her warm.

HIKING ON SNOW

I f you take your children hiking on snow, you must provide protection from sunburn and snow blindness. Safe behind their sunglasses, adults can easily misjudge the intensity of the sun's rays reflected up from the snow. These reflected rays are a real menace; they can cause snow blindness and even burns on the roof of the mouth and up the nostrils. A sunburned child can become seriously ill. Guard your child's face and neck with a sun hat; protect her nose and mouth with a scarf or bandanna. Watch out for "burn gaps" between sleeve cuffs and mitten cuffs, and between pant legs and socks. An older child may tolerate sun goggles, such as skiers and climbers wear, but don't send your child out with children's sunglasses from the variety store; most of them are worthless toys. Make sure that the sunglasses offer real protection. Many babies won't accept goggles on their faces, so never take the risk of hiking on snow in full sun with a baby, unless she is covered above, on all sides, and below. An application of sunscreen to the child's face will screen out the burning rays, but some parents don't like to use any creams or lotions on their children's skin; those parents rely entirely on clothing to keep the sun off.

DEHYDRATION

S ome of the symptoms of *hyperthermia*—overheating and dehydration during strenuous exercise—are similar to those of hypothermia: muscle weakness, stumbling, mental confusion. The two conditions are opposites. Hyperthermia is caused by a loss of fluids through sweating; hikers experience hyperthermia when they are carrying heavy loads up steep hills on warm days, so it is likely that parents will be affected before their children are. The best way to avoid hyperthermia is to drink plenty of good, plain water, before, during, and after hiking. Sugary drinks take longer to be absorbed in the intestine than plain water, and salty, alcoholic, and caffeine drinks pull fluid from your cells and make you more dehydrated.

There is an old wives' or old hikers' tale that insists that salt tablets are the remedy for overheating, to replace the salt lost through excessive sweating. Salt—more precisely sodium—is already present in large amounts in many of the foods that back-packers eat, such as cheeses, crackers, peanut butter, canned or dried meats and fish, and prepackaged hiking foods; this salt is more than enough to replace lost salt. Even the salt in foods pulls fluids from your body, so food should always be eaten with water, and if you add extra salt to your diet, then you should be drinking even more water.

HIKING IN THE DESERT

By Arizona statute, it is a crime to refuse anyone a drink of water; that's how seriously Southwesterners take desert conditions. Everything in this book pertaining to exposure to sun or dehydration—wearing long sleeves, long pants, wide-brimmed hats; drinking lots of water—holds true. Begin drinking water two hours before you begin hiking; take a good drink every 15 minutes. Don't wait until you feel thirsty; by that time, you're already beginning to be dehydrated. See that everyone in your party drinks, too. If you see signs of dehydration, give water or a fluid replacement beverage like Gatorade®, but avoid dehydrating drinks. Carry lots of water, and don't count on finding water sources on the trail unless you have been reliably informed of their location.

Sun and heat are the problems during the day, but at night it may be the cold that you must plan for. Again, inquire locally about conditions before you set out, and be aware that even in spring or fall there may be sudden snow storms.

DANGEROUS CRITTERS

When you enter a wilderness area, you are entering the homes of the creatures that already live there. Teach your children to respect those creatures. Try to prevent a hostile encounter with a dangerous critter. Tell your children never to put a hand or a foot under a log or a rock; or poke a stick into a hole in a log. If you see a snake or some other critter, don't tease it; let it escape. (Even if it's harmless, like a slug, don't torture it.) Teach your children to look before they sit down to see what they might be sitting on or near. Have everyone in your party wear a bell to warn the wild animals that you are coming into their territory. Be sure that everyone in your party wears sturdy boots.

The desert holds special fears for many people through tales of rattlesnakes, scorpions, and Gila monsters. Study a first-aid manual for your area before you set out, so you know what to do if someone in your group is bitten or stung. Tell your children to move away if they hear a rattle. Most scorpions are not poisonous; still, it's a good idea to shake out your shoes each morning before you put them on. The Gila monster is the only poisonous lizard in the US. It is notorious for locking on to the prey it bites. If that is the limb of a person in your group, force the lizard to open its jaws with a stick or hold a flame under its jaw or immerse the limb and the Gila monster in water.

If you are wearing a bell, any bears in your vicinity should not be surprised when you meet them. If the bear is ahead of you on the trail, back away slowly. Do not run. Some people say you should try not to appear hostile; clasp your hands in front of you and bow your head. Some advocate talking quietly to the bear: "Don't be frightened, I'm not going to hurt you." If the bear approaches, some people advise crouching or playing dead. Bears are unpredictable, and I am no expert. The bears I have encountered on the trail seemed to be just as scared as I was, and they ran away from me! A bear who comes into camp is a different kind of animal, one who has probably experienced human food or garbage and is looking for more. Shout at the bear, bang a rock against a cooking pan, back away if the bear continues to advance. Do not throw rocks or antagonize the bear. Be sure to stow your food in the most bear-proof way that you can.

A Latin American legend says that a child may sleep safely in the open where the mountain lion is the only wild animal around. I don't believe it! As the mountain lion (which is called a *cougar* in the Northwest and a *puma* or a *panther* in other parts of the country) has been displaced by humans encroaching on its territory, it has become more and more bold. Mountain lions hunt by stalking small prey and pouncing on them. Newspaper reports of cougars attacking children are rare, but they occur. Not long ago, a cougar attacked a child playing near a stream in British Columbia. The boy's mother drove the big cat off with her walking stick. If a mountain lion approaches your camp, don't crouch. Make yourself look as big as you can. Raise your arms, shout, and brandish a stick. Don't rush at it unless it actually attacks one of your party. Then go after it with the stick.

FIRE

Like so many other hazards in the backcountry, fire can sometimes be prevented. Many forest fires start in campgrounds, from campfires that were left unattended or abandoned. Leaking fuel and carelessness with matches have started fires even where stoves were required instead of open fires. Teach your children by example to be careful with matches and fires, and to place their stoves on bare dirt or rock. If you are out in the woods and you see smoke or fire where it shouldn't be, it's best to head out by the nearest trail. If you obtained a permit or signed the register at the trailhead, or if you left word of your whereabouts with a home guard, the authorities will know there are campers in a risky area and will try to send word to evacuate (another good reason for leaving word).

LYME DISEASE

Although this disease was first identified in Old Lyme, Connecticut, cases of Lyme disease have been seen in all parts of the country. Symptoms include a rash, high fever, headaches, chills, and painful joints. Lethargy, fatigue, or arthritis-like pain may persist for many months. If not treated, Lyme disease may evolve into a much more serious second stage as meningitis, paralysis, or abnormal heart beat. A third stage, which can occur years later, may mimic multiple sclerosis or chronic arthritis.

Insect repellents—"deet," for example—will deter the tiny deer tick that carries Lyme disease, but repellents have dangers of their own (see Insect Repellents, pp. 99-101). What should conscientious parents do? For starters, avoid areas where the disease-bearing ticks have been reported. Further good advice: dress your child in long pants with the pant legs tucked into high socks; inspect members of your party frequently for ticks; use repellent sparingly on clothing, and even more sparingly on children's exposed skin (but never under clothing). Inspect your children's bodies for ticks when you put them to bed, and also when they get up.

If you find a tick, you should remove it. The current favored method is to grasp the embedded tick with tweezers or a tick removal device as close to the skin as you can. Pull it out steadily; do not jerk or twist. Take care not to crush the tick or get any fluids on your hands. Wipe the entry point with alcohol or the disinfectant in your first-aid kit; wash your hands with soap and water.If you or your children show symptoms associated with Lyme disease, be sure to tell your doctor when and where you might have been exposed to the ticks. (For more about ticks, read Roger Drummond's *Ticks and What You Can Do About Them*, Wilderness Press).

THE LAST CHAPTER

Most books on backpacking end with a plea to respect the environment that you are visiting, to preserve it for the future. The classic warning is, "Take nothing but pictures, leave nothing but footprints." That is good advice, but this book has a different message.

If someone created a special tee-shirt to wear while backpacking with babies and small children, the front of the shirt could say, "Experienced parents have learned," while the back should read, "Use your own good head." Conflicting? No. Those two phrases summarize the principles of family hiking. In other words, before you set out, learn as much as you can about what other families do (by reading this book and by asking hikers you know), and then apply that knowledge to your own family. Start out doing things the way other people do them, and then gradually develop your own style. That way you will begin your excursions safely, staying well within your family's limitations and using tested techniques. As you build up your skills, you can undertake increasingly difficult adventures.

Have fun together. Don't worry about accomplishing record-breaking feats, but concentrate instead on personal triumphs. Enjoy one another's company and savor the world around you.

Then when your children grow up, having come to know the mountains and forests, they may take their own children backpacking and teach them what they learned from you. If we are concerned about preserving what we have for future generations, then we must bring up future generations who will care for what they inherit. If your children can learn to care about one forest, one stream, they may begin to care about the whole world, to be concerned with preserving it. The legacy that you give your children in the backcountry can be far more valuable than any other inheritance you leave them.

Maybe this book is not so different from the others after all.

APPENDIX A: What To Take

Every family will develop its own list of equipment to take hiking. The sample list that follows illustrates one family's choices. The items in italics will apply only if the family has someone in diapers or still using baby bottles.

EVERYONE IN THE FAMILY WILL WEAR:

Underwear
Long-sleeved shirt
Sturdy pants
Good hiking shoes and socks
Diapers and waterproof covers
Hat

FOR A DAY HIKE, THEY WILL TAKE:

TO WEAR:

Gloves and mittens
Parka
Sweater
Rainwear
Diapers and extra waterproof covers
Extra pants (for newly toilet-trained youngsters)
Extra socks
Extra mittens (in wet weather)

TO USE:

Tissues or handkerchiefs
Premoistened towelettes
Toilet paper
Sun block
Insect repellent
Diaper-changing materials
Plastic bags
Pocket knife

Map
Compass
Garbage bags

TO EAT:

Cups
Spoons
Baby bottles
Powdered milk
Powdered fruit drink
Lunch
Snacks

TO SURVIVE:

First-aid kit
Whistles
Fire starter
Nylon fishing line (for repairs)
Needle and thread
Safety pins
Tarp or emergency blanket
Rope
Sunglasses
Flashlight and spare batteries
Matches
Canteens (filled with water)

OPTIONALS

Camera and film
Small toys
Security blanket

FOR AN OVERNIGHTER, THEY WILL TAKE EVERYTHING ABOVE AND ADD:

TO WEAR:

Long johns or warm pajamas
More diapers
Blanket sleeper

TO USE:

Comb
Toothbrushes and toothpaste
Soap
Towel and wash cloth
Wash basin

TO EAT:

Dinner
Breakfast
Stove
Fuel
Can-opener, if your knife doesn't have one
Cooking pans and utensils
Dish towel
Detergent
Scouring pad

TO SLEEP:

Tent with poles, stakes, and rain fly
Sleeping bags
Insulating pads or mattresses
Pack covers

APPENDIX B: Mail-Order Sources

The stores and manufacturers listed below all offer mail-order service or information. Call or write to them about your special needs or to obtain their catalogues.

BABY BUNZ & CO.
PO Box 113
Lynden, WA 98264
(800) 676-4559
FAX 1-360-354-1203
Waterproof diaper covers that are not plastic, deluxe cotton diapers of many shapes and styles, other baby items in natural fibers

BABYWORKS
11725 N.W. West Road
Portland, OR 97229
(800) 422-2910 / (503) 645-4349
"Environmentally-kind Baby Products," diapers and diaper covers, rainwear

BABY WRAP PRODUCTS, INC
P.O. Box 100584, Dept. O
Denver, CO 80250-0584
(800) 432-0494
"A baby carrier adapted from a traditional African design."

L. L. BEAN, INC
Freeport, ME 04033
(800) 221-4221
FAX 1-207-552-3080
Shop On-Line: www.llbean.com
L.L.Kids is a special catalogue of bright, sturdy clothing for infants, toddlers, and larger children, and also shoes, packs, underwear, and outerwear that is windproof, waterproof, and warm.

CAMPMOR
PO Box 700-J
Saddle River, N.J. 07458-0700
(800) 226-7667
Don't be put off by the cheap paper or the lack of colored photos.
This little catalogue offers a wide variety of children's clothing,
shoes, and equipment, many at discounted prices. Grown-up
stuff, too.

DIAPER DOUBLERS
(800) 545 1239
Disposable pads to lay on a diaper to make it more absorbent.
Call for the retail outlet closest to you.

EVENFLO® (Gerry® and Snugli®)
(800) 233 5921
In 1998, Evenflo acquired the Gerry® line of baby carriers,
including the Snugli®, soft baby carriers in several styles and a
variety of materials. Call if you have difficulty finding those
products.

GERBER BABY PRODUCTS
(800) 443-7237
Flat-fold and pre-folded cloth diapers in gauze or birdseye. E Z
Liners®, a paper diaper liner. Call for their nearest outlet. Gerber
will accept direct orders at retail price if there is none in your
area, so as not to compete with their retailers.

MOUNTAIN MASTERS
P.O. Box 1631
Grass Valley, CA 95945
(916) 273-0769
(Toddler Tote, a luxurious, carefully engineered baby carrier.)

MALDEN MILLS OUTLET STORES
For general information about Polarfleece®, Polartec®, and other
Malden products, call (800) 252-6688.
> SEATTLE OUTLET STORE
> 2401 Utah Ave S., Suite 160
> Seattle WA 98134
> (206) 682-7037

LAWERENCE OUTLET STORE
530 Broadway
Lawrence, MA 01842
(978) 557-3242 or 557-3246

NORDSTROM
1501 Fifth Avenue
Seattle, WA 98101
(206) 628-2111, extension 1460
Write or call collect for children's shoes.

PANGRAPHICS
937 East Browning Ave.
Salt Lake City, UT 84105
(801) 467-3240
A choice of six different colored bandannas printed with identifiable animal tracks or skat.

QUANTUM, INC
754 Washington St
Eugene, OR 97401
(800) 448-1448
Call to find your local source for these all-natural products: Buzz Away™, insect repellent lotion, insect repellent-sunscreen, and individual towelettes; also Itch Nix™ and Sting Soother™.)

RAINY PASS REPAIR, INC.
5307 Roosevelt Way N.E.
Seattle, WA 98105
(888) Rip-Stop or (206) 523-8135
E-mail: ripstop@eskimo.net
Will repair or modify any pack.

REI (Recreational Equipment, Inc.)
1700 45th St. E.
Sumner, WA 98390
(800) 426-4840
E-mail: www.rei.com
The grand-daddy of all outdoor stores, now with more than 60 retail stores. Call or write for the store nearest you, or to place mail orders or for a catalogue. You will often find merchandise in the stores that is not in the catalogue.

SEATTLE FABRICS
Karen Christianson
8702 Aurora Ave. N.
Seattle, WA 98103
(206) 525-0670
FAX (206) 525-0779
Outdoor and recreational fabrics of all kinds, and patterns for outdoor clothing, including kids' wear.

TARMEGAN
2134 N. 86th St.
Seattle, WA 98103
(206) 729-7218
E-mail: tarmegan@aol.com
Raingear and fleece clothing that KIDS WEAR!™. Owners Megan and Tim Ratcliffe were extremely helpful to me in writing the sections on kids' clothes.

TOUGH TRAVELER®
1012 State St.
Schenectady, N.Y. 12307
(518) 377-8526
FAX (518) 377-5434
Sturdy child carriers in many styles, with optional accessories; kid-sized packs; Caper and Macaw rain capes to wear in a carrier; Baby Bear and Growing Bear modular sleeping bag.

SWALLOWS NEST
3320 Meridian Ave N
Seattle, WA 98103
(206) 633-0408
A growing children's department; rainwear, down vests, wool and fleece clothing, polypropylene underwear, all in a range of sizes; children's sunglasses and gaiters; coming soon: children's hiking boots in leather and nylon combination.

TAYMOR LEISURE PRODUCTS
43 Park Lane
Brisbane, CA 94005
(415) 467-1010
Outbound Baby Carrier, lightweight, rugged, deluxe carrier.

APPENDIX C: Recommended Reading

Your public library is a treasury of information that will make your hiking more enjoyable and informative. An afternoon's browsing in one neighborhood library turned up these good books. You can find lots more yourself.

BACKPACKING BOOKS

The Complete Walker, Colin Fletcher, Knopf.

Backpacking: One Step At A Time, Harvey Manning, Random House.

Backpacking Basics, Thomas Winnett and Melanie Findling, Wilderness Press.

Beginning Backpacking, Tony Freeman, Children's Press.
A book full of colored photographs that you can read to your preschoolers to prepare them for their first hike or overnight outing.

How to Shit in the Woods, Kathleen Meyer, Ten Speed Press.
An environmentally sound approach to a lost art.

FIRST-AID BOOKS

Emergency Medical Procedures for the Backpacker, Patient Care Publications, Arco.

Mountaineering Medicine, Fred T. Darvill, M.D., Wilderness Press.

SAFETY

Willie Takes a Hike, Gloria Rand, illustrated by Ted Rand, Harcourt Brace.
Willie gets lost, but this book tells him what to do.

Ticks and What You Can Do About Them, Roger Drummond, M.D., Wilderness Press

GAMES

Games (and More!) for Backpackers, June Fleming, Victoria House.
Finger Fun, Songs & Rhythms for the Very Young, Helen Wright Salisbury, Cowman Publications.
Finger Plays for Nursery & Kindergarten, Emilie Poulsson, Dover Publications (a reproduction of a book published in Boston in 1893).
Sing Hey Diddle Diddle 66 Nursery Rhymes and Their Traditional Tunes, and *Count Me In, 44 Songs & Rhymes About Numbers,* both from A & C Black, London.

WILD FLOWERS

In the juvenile section, I found:
Wild Flowers, Viola K. Beaudoin, Evergreen Company.
Wildflowers & the Stories Behind Their Names, Phillis S. Busch, Scribner.
Weeds & Wild Flowers, Illa Podendorf, Children's Press.
—but it is probably wisest to find a wildflower book for your own region.

   In addition, the Boy Scouts, Girl Scouts, and Camp Fire Girls and Boys all publish numerous books on campcraft, backpacking, nature, songs, etc. Also look for books that describe rock collecting, identifying animals and animal tracks, birds, fishing, geology, and wild edibles in the area you live in, and other books on subjects of local lore such as history, Indians, and early exploration.
   For information on the Garbage Project, contact the Bureau of Applied Research in Anthropology, Department of Anthropology, University of Arizona, Tucson, AZ 85721. Phone (520) 621 6299. William Rathje is the founder and director of the Garbage Project.
   And don't forget to have the librarian order: A Comparative Study of Frameless Baby Carrier Designs and Development of a Pattern Intended for Home Use, a Thesis for the Degree of Master of Science in Home Economics and Family Studies by Catherine Mary Jeffris, Central Washington University, Ellensburg, Washington.

ACKNOWLEDGMENTS

I am grateful to the people whose expertise and photographs made this book and the first and second editions possible. They are: Jeff Berman, Josette Pelletier, and Sahale Pelletier; L. L. Bean; Leslie, Michael, and Joshua Boguch; Goldie Caughlin; Karen Christianson, Seattle Fabrics; Cathy, Ted, and Jeff Cooley; Jim, Ginny, and Jeff Evans; Karen, Steve, and Eric Fry; Cliff Godwin, Cathy Reiner Godwin, Shaina and Kendra Godwin; Nancy Gold of Tough Traveler; Lois, Jeff, and Matthew Hancock; Poppi S. and Hillary Handy; Cathy Jeffris; Timothy Jones, the Garbage Project; Charlene and Margaret Hope Kahn; Yonah Karp and Hannah Bobroff; Wendy Marcus; Ann Marshall; Louise Marshall; Frederica Overstreet, Gordon Hicks, and Robert Hicks; Tim and Megan Ratcliffe, Tarmegan; Ron, Rhonda, and Adam Robb; Judy Roberts; Ed Schreiner; Bob, Delilah, and Samantha Simon; Jonathan, Robert, Rena, and Jenny Singer; John Stevely; Ray Smutek; David, Kathy, Kevin and Peter Tempest; Doug, Mitsi, Chris and Kelli Vondrachek; Chuck Wiese; Scott Walker; Rob and Sammy Zisette; the readers of Pack & Paddle and Signpost for Northwest Trails; these national park rangers: Larry Lang, Eli Warren, and Dan Johnson; and of course all the Silvermans—Don, John, Judy, Jeff, Judith, Sarah, and Daniel.

INDEX